THE FIRM'S SENSITIVITY TO THE SITING AND ORIENTATION OF ITS BUILDIN[...] STRUCTURES THAT MINIMIZE TH[...] SOUTHWESTERN SUMMER HEAT AND PROVIDE VENTILATION FROM THE PREVAILING BREEZES. EQUALLY, THE BUILDINGS PROVIDE FOR WINTER SUNLIGHT AND SOLAR HEAT GAIN, MINIMIZING THE SEASONAL CONSUMPTION OF ENERGY.

THE WORK DRAWS FROM RELEVANT HISTORIC LOW-TECHNOLOGY SOLUTIONS AND AVOIDS THE PICTURESQUE. THOUGHTFUL, DIRECT, CLEAR, AND STRONG, IT IS AN HONEST, NO-NONSENSE ARCHITECTURE. LAKE|FLATO HAS PURSUED IDEALS WITH INTEGRITY THROUGH RESPECT FOR NATURE AND A RECOGNITION OF THE GENIUS OF PLACE.

LAKE|FLATO'S BODY OF WORK IS MODERN YET NOT SENSATIONAL. MANY PROJECTS POSSESS THAT ALL-TOO-RARE QUALITY OF SERENITY.

IT IS SIMPLE AND JOYOUS ARCHITECTURE, ROOTED WITHIN THE REGIONS TO WHICH IT BELONGS.

—GLENN MURCUTT, HFAIA,
PRITZKER PRIZE LAUREATE, 2002

LAKE | FLATO

BUILDINGS & LANDSCAPES

edited by oscar riera ojeda
foreword by glenn murcutt
introduction by thomas fisher

rockport publishers

FLAT

HILLSIDE

TRANSITIONAL

URBAN

LAKE | FLATO

BUILDINGS

LANDSCAPES

edited by Oscar Riera Ojeda
foreword by Glen Murcott
introduction by Thomas Fisher

Rockport Publishers

CONTENTS

FLAT

HILLSIDE

Vernacular Values   The work of Lake/Flato returns architecture to its roots, reminding us of how humans have long made shelter. Their buildings adapt to the climate by opening up to breezes and views, often with broad doors that give rooms direct access outside. Their architecture uses locally quarried stone and regionally made products, preserving the essence of each place. The firm's structures adjust to the terrain of each site, with as little disturbance to the landscape as possible. With remarkably durable construction and substantial materials, Lake/Flato designs buildings to last.

Their architecture stands out in a construction industry that wastes tremendous amounts of energy and resources, viewing buildings as investments, abstractions on balance sheets rather than as real places in which we live and work. Lake/Flato reveals what we are missing with this skewed view of buildings. Their work shows how we might begin to construct a more sustainable physical environment, through an economy of means and enduring form.

The design work of the firm begins with the land on which it typically builds: the semi-arid prairie of west Texas; the rocky hills of central Texas; the grassy scrublands of south Texas; the wooded wetlands of coastal Texas; as well as the dark bayous of Louisiana, the intense desert of New Mexico, and the dramatic terrain of the Colorado Rockies.

Lake/Flato, whose offices occupy a former car showroom one block from the Alamo in downtown San Antonio, works not just in rural locations, but also in urban centers and at the transitions between man-made and natural environments. In each of these places, Lake/Flato's buildings do not just occupy the land, but also respect, reinforce, and repair it. "We try to improve every place we build," says David Lake, "leaving the environment better than we found it."

Adapting to the local climate also plays a big part in Lake/Flato's work. The firm frequently breaks a building down into pavilions around courtyards to encourage cross ventilation and capture outdoor living space. With broad overhangs and metal roofs to shade windows and reflect the sun, Lake/Flato also takes full advantage of slopes

and adjacent bodies of water to induce air movement and a cool breeze through their buildings. And they orient their structures toward the sun and prevailing winds to naturally heat and cool the interiors as much as possible.

Even in urban areas, the firm manages to make the best of local climatic conditions by capturing outdoor space within or between buildings, setting up cooler microclimates within the larger heat sink of cities. For example, connecting buildings with canopies and colonnades. Such strategies recall those common before the widespread use of central heating and cooling. They are all newly relevant today, with our need to reduce dependence on fossil fuels.

Lake/Flato is not alone in this concern about the land and climate. But very few firms with this orientation handle materials and details with the same conviction and elegance. Lake/Flato, for instance, often uses huge slabs of stone, laid up in blocks like some bit of ancient construction remaining on the site. This comes from their interest in the effect of time and weathering on their buildings. "We like the question our mentor, O'Neil Ford, used to ask about the permanence of design," says Lake, "'What will your building look like as a ruin?' It was a way that he used to question the weathering and timeless character of the design." Lake/Flato have built some of the most beautiful future-ruins of our time.

Other elements commonly found in their buildings – timber structures, stone flooring, metal cladding, screened enclosures, copper walls – all get handled in ways that recall the solidity of traditional construction. Materials always turn corners, walls usually have depth, and connections often get expressed. "We try to strip away things," says Flato, "to get to essentials, in as straightforward and practical a way as possible." Most of the materials used – local stone, regional products, and wood sometimes even harvested on the site - come from the places in which they work. This not only connects their buildings to their locations, but also heals the land by reducing the impact on the natural world while supporting regional economies.

Behind this lies a deep connection on the part of Lake/Flato to local cultures. This stems, in part, from the careers of the firm's founding partners, David Lake and Ted Flato. After graduating from architecture school – the University of Texas, Austin, in Lake's case, and Stanford University in Flato's – they took various paths until, in 1980, they wound up working together in the San Antonio office of O'Neil Ford. Ford was a modernist architect ahead of his time in recognizing the importance of local climate and regional culture, and in refusing to divorce modern architecture from the past.

Ford died in 1982, and Lake and Flato started their own firm in 1984. With eight partners and a staff of more than 50 employees, the firm has won over 100 local

and regional design awards, and has gained a growing national presence, earning several national AIA honor awards, and in 2004, the American Institute of Architect's prestigious Firm Award.

Despite the professional and media attention they have attracted, Lake/Flato remain rooted in the traditional culture of Texas and the Southwest. "We admire the practicality of ranchers," says Flato, "using the materials at hand in a spare, simple way." Other "rancher" values embodied in Lake/Flato's work include frugality and ingenuity, inventiveness and restraint—values that are both aesthetic and ethical in nature, finding their clearest expression in the rapidly disappearing older buildings of small towns and rural landscapes.

In their appreciation of the practical solutions of vernacular architecture, Lake/Flato reveals a particularly American way of thinking. In traditional and resource-strapped cultures, people make do with what they have available to them. But only in America did that practice become a philosophy - pragmatism - characterized by experimentation, a lack of formality, a concern with the consequences of human actions, and a willingness to go with what works, regardless of how it might appear to others.

This pragmatism is evident in the humble working buildings that Lake/Flato so admires: ranches and farm buildings, old factories and commercial structures, hunting lodges and fishing shacks. Pragmatism also drives the mix of seemingly opposite qualities in their work: experimental, but also respectful of tradition; informal, but also revealing an underlying formal order; materially elegant, while also embodying a working-person's soul.

Of course, many architects have a pragmatic bent and an admiration of vernacular architecture. But what sets the work of Lake/Flato apart is the deep, humble character of their buildings, recalling the best work of their mentors, O'Neil Ford and William Turnbull, and of other critical regionalists they admire, like Peter Zumthor, Glenn Murcutt, and Alvaro Siza. Because of the range of influences, Lake/Flato's architecture reflects no single, signature style. What ties their work together, instead, is a common sensibility, one that sees environmental sustainability, cultural traditions, and architectural aesthetics as inseparable. In an age that has pushed the natural environment to near exhaustion, relegated cultural traditions to theme parks, and dismissed architectural aesthetics as irrelevant, that sensibility is one we need more of, more often.

Lake/Flato's sensible, non-stylistic approach leads to common characteristics in many of their buildings. The firm often highlights important program elements as pavilions amidst connecting "service" spaces, and emphasizes the thickness of walls sometimes to

the point of their enclosing whole rooms. They like to break down the divisions between indoor and outdoor spaces, moving whole parts of a program outside whenever possible. They will also create axial relationships among spaces in a building to tie them together, and play with the scale of buildings by partly burying structures into hillsides, to make them seem smaller, or by increasing the size of elements, such as masonry, to make them seem larger. These features give Lake/Flato's buildings an incredibly evocative quality that speaks to our memory and imagination.

Indeed, they speak an architectural language that we have almost forgotten. "As we do our work," says Lake, "it often feels like remembering lost dialects," so disconnected have we all become from the land and the local cultures that had adapted over time to particular climates. Some may shrug at that loss, seeing only good in a single, global culture. But, like the rapid loss of the world's diverse spoken languages, these built dialects have embedded in them strategies for living comfortably in particular places. The gradual disappearance of locally adapted vernacular buildings makes it harder for us to achieve a more sustainable future. We have literally forgotten how to build responsibly and live appropriately in different places.

Some think that keeping alive such traditional architectural languages constitutes a form of nostalgia, and it can be if we treat them as something cute, as a comforting veneer to cover up how much we have actually forgotten. But Lake/Flato's architecture is anything but nostalgic. To the firm, rediscovering and reviving traditional forms of adaptation to local climate and culture constitute a form of survival, a way in which humans will be able to live once the oil wells and water wells begin to run dry.

This book, divided into four parts, shows how Lake/Flato pursue these ideas in four very different settings. Many of their buildings occupy flat, featureless landscapes, be they deserts, prairies, or the sprawl of farm fields or edge cities. In such places, the architecture has to create an oasis, protection from the heat, and shade from the sun. Lake/Flato also work in very dramatic sites, on steeply sloping terrains, in deep mountain valleys, on stark rocky hillsides, and in heavily forested settings, where anchorage against and exposure to the surroundings become the dual task of the architecture. At the same time, Lake/Flato frequently build in transitional locations, where the built environment meets the natural world, and where the architecture has to form an edge, boundary, or filter between one and the other. In extremely fragile urban landscapes, their buildings have an obligation to repair, bridge, connect, and infill the gaps in such places, while providing a contrast to the urban environment. Wherever they work, Lake/Flato brings to that

place a common sensibility, one that honors the land and its resources, the local culture and climate.

As we look ahead to a global environment in which scarcity will once again characterize the existence of many people, the architecture of Lake/Flato shows us a possible way forward. Their work demonstrates that beauty and sustainability are not mutually exclusive and that our future depends upon our rediscovering how we once built and what we once valued: humility and honesty, respect and restraint.

—THOMAS FISHER

FLAT

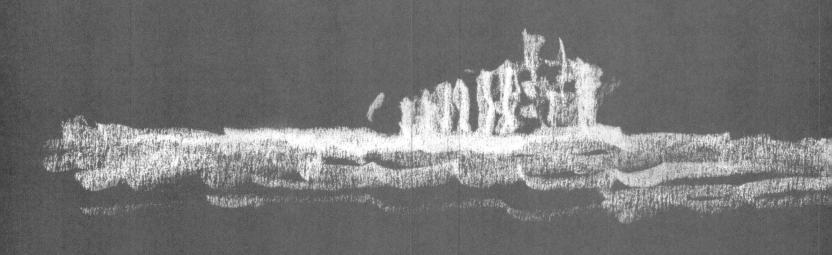

Lake | Flato works in a number of flat, desolate landscapes that offer long views, little shelter, and a lot of exposure to wind and sun. Ranging from isolated desert and prairie locations to the far edges of cities and suburbs, these places demand a great deal from the buildings. The architecture of flat landscapes acknowledge the openness of their surroundings, while offering a degree of protection from it: large, deeply inset windows to take advantage of views and enclosed outdoor spaces to provide respite from the intense climate.

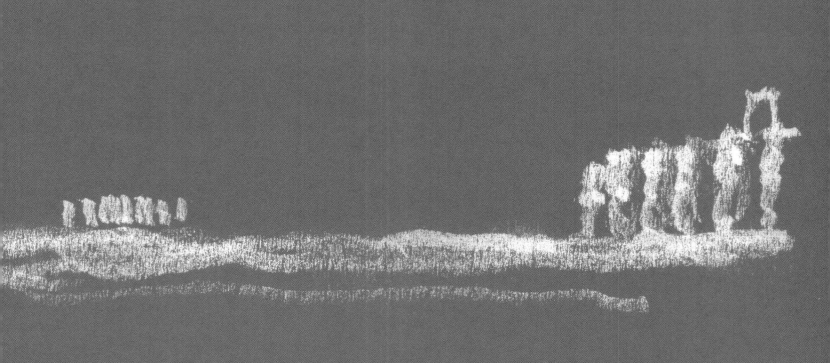

In contrast to the boundlessness of landscape, the buildings create edges and boundaries, with thick walls and carefully framed views. Without the presence of trees, structures have to shade themselves with broad overhangs and covered walkways. Of Lake | Flato's work, the buildings in flat landscapes hew most closely to vernacular architecture of the region – with their simple sheds and courtyard buildings - due to its suitability to harsh sites and climates. These are welcome places of refuge, places you want to retreat to and stay.

HOUSE OF LIGHT

Art looks best in natural light, although too much daylight destroys art, a paradox as true for architecture as it is for paintings. This house for an art collector shows how architecture can become a light filter, letting in enough light for people to see the true colors of the art without harming it in the process. Lake/Flato accomplished this by treating the main gallery as a partly sunken, central room, surrounded by other living spaces that buffer all direct light. A greenhouse off the gallery also adds humidity and fragrance. A wall wraps around the perimeter of the house, creating an outdoor court that serves as a sculpture garden, while the thickness of the wall further shelters the house from the direct sun, which is essential in the desert climate of Santa Fe. Architecture, as much art, benefits from the control of light in this elegantly minimalist house.

Santa Fe, New Mexico
1996

The low horizontal gallery intersects the tall vertical gallery (above). Typical Santa Fe adobe walls used as reference (above left).

Simple cubist massing recalls pueblo architecture (above); light arcs upon the adobe mass wall (bottom right).

The freestanding adobe wall serves as thermal mass, absorbing heat from the solarium while bouncing light into the gallery (above).

DESERT HOUSE

We live in desert climates because of the sun and warm weather. At the same time, we seek shelter from their intensity. This house, located in the open desert near Santa Fe, New Mexico, "works like a sun dial," say clients Sally and Tom Dunning, encouraging them to migrate to various outdoor "portals," depending upon the time of day or year. The "morning portal" faces southwest, the "evening portal" northwest, and the "winter portal" south. These porch-like elements connect six stuccoed Donald Judd-like blocks that surround a walled courtyard, with an open-air covered walk connecting them. Each block contains a major room—garage, bedrooms, and living/dining room—with service areas—kitchen, bathrooms, and storage—occupying the "walls" around them. The blocks and their thick enclosures also serve as blinders, shading the glass walls and sheltering the recessed portals. With its Mission plan of rooms around a cloister, the house shows the form-giving power of climate, especially one as severe as the desert.

Santa Fe, New Mexico
2003

The shading and editing nature of the minimalist sculpture of Donald Judd (above) helped influence the design of the house.

1. Entry Portal　2. Courtyard　3. Living/Dining　4. Bedroom　5. Kitchen

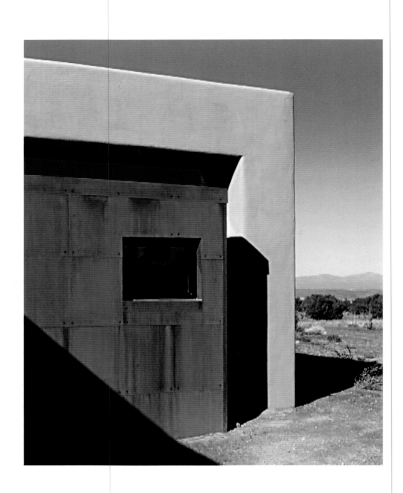

The massive stucco forms are contrasted with light, rusted steel porches and breezeways.

Service elements are concealed by thick walls which frame views and admit glare free light.

Concrete floors, counters, and tub with plaster walls; a simple palette of materials (above).

Local wooden barns supplied inspiration (above). Recycled oil field pipe is used on other outbuildings (top).

AIR BARNS

People have architectural needs, and so do animals, as these two horse barns demonstrate. Sited along the edges of two open, sunny polo fields, the barns create a shady, cool home for both horses and riders. Built of recycled, rusted oil field pipe, an indigenous material, the barns maximize shade while capturing the prevailing cool, coastal breezes with open, airy interiors, generous eight-foot overhangs, and continuous ridge vents. The partition system, with walls of wooden slats, provides each horse with individual space, while maintaining a communal sense of the herd on the open range. More solid shed-roof forms, with rolling barn doors for access, flank both ends of the stalls. The east shed is the feed room (or kitchen) and the west shed contains the tack room (or closets) storing all required equine gear. These barns offer a good example of the sensitivity Lake/Flato often display towards the needs of their clients and, in this case, the needs of horses.

San Saba, Texas
1998

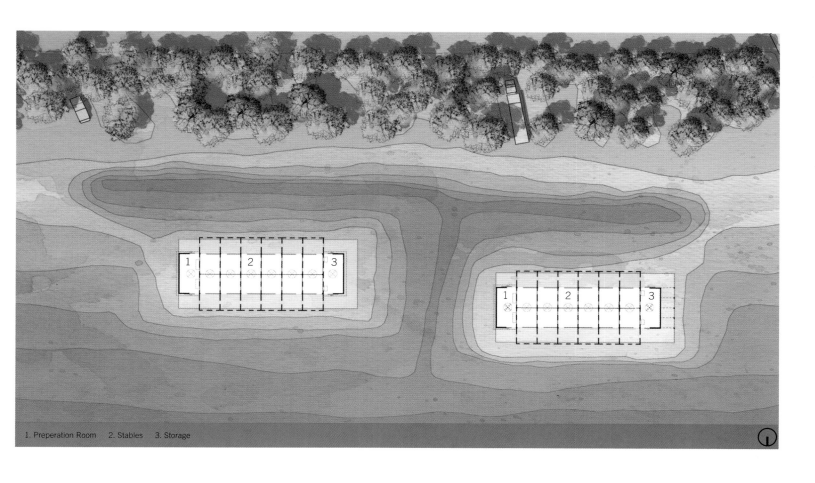

1. Preperation Room   2. Stables   3. Storage

Exposed steel frame becomes the armature for ranch-tech cabinets in the closed sheds.

The architects capitalized on the local welding tradition of the area by building the barns with recycled oil field pipe.

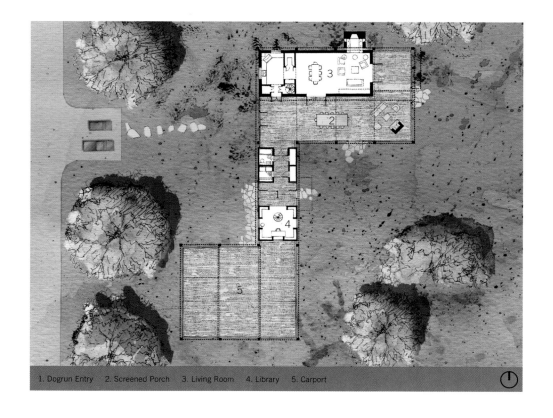

1. Dogrun Entry 2. Screened Porch 3. Living Room 4. Library 5. Carport

ALAMO CEMENT HOUSE

Frugality can lead to remarkable freedom, as this house shows. On a fourty-acre river-bottom site, the house reuses the steel frame, stair rails, and ventilators of a decommissioned cement plant bought for $20,000. The clients, Henry and Francine Carraro, had a modest budget, but big dreams. The architects re-erected the 40' x 180' steel-framed building into a "Z" shape around existing oak trees, with an open carport, a two-story, metal-clad library and master bedroom, and a huge screened-in living area. Enclosed within this great screened "room" is a limestone box housing the air-conditioned living room, dining room, and kitchen with a guest suite above. The stone building, with a walk-in fireplace alcove, shields the house from winter winds, while funneling summer breezes from the southeast. The horizontal framing for the porch's screening celebrates the flat landscape and makes the large volume feel smaller. The recycled cement plant resulted in a 6,400 sq. ft. house, built for $200,000—an excellent example of how leaving nothing to waste can lead to an enlargement of liberty.

Kyle, Texas
1990

The house was built with salvaged materials from the demolished 1930's Alamo Cement Plant.

Flat steel siding, corrugated metal siding, salvaged steel trusses and Texas limestone.

The house integrates a variety of recycled elements from the demolished cement plant: kiln bricks at fireplace, hand rails from a generator, and steel framing from a toolshed.

1. Breezeway & Entry   2. Store / Restaraunt   3. Exhibits   4. Office   5. Wetland Court   6. Arid Court   7. Irrigation Canal

BIRDING CENTER

Remarkable feats of engineering, birds' nests use available materials, recycle older nests, and biodegrade when no longer needed. This center for the study of birds in the Rio Grande delta suggests what the human equivalent of a bird's nest might be. Lake/Flato located the center's long, narrow structures adjacent to an irrigation canal and restored the bird habitat by reclaiming the abandoned onion field and mending the land to create this natural oasis in the Tamaulipan Desert. Oriented in an east/west direction, the long, vaulted buildings conserve energy, while creating a series of courtyards for a variety of habitats. Arched Quonset hut roofs, common on local farm buildings, provide 32-foot clear spans, below which stand clay-tile-clad structures that enclose office and visitor facilities. Recycled materials and high-efficiency, low-energy systems abound in the buildings, whose roofs funnel rainwater to corner cisterns to irrigate the gardens. Ample day lighting and flexible spaces also allow for a variety of activities, while reducing the buildings' size and cost. Humans have yet to match the elegance and efficiency of a bird's building skills, but this low-impact birding center comes pretty close.

Agri-tech steel vaults, mission stone vaults, and the Kimbell Museum inspired this design.

Mission, Texas
2004

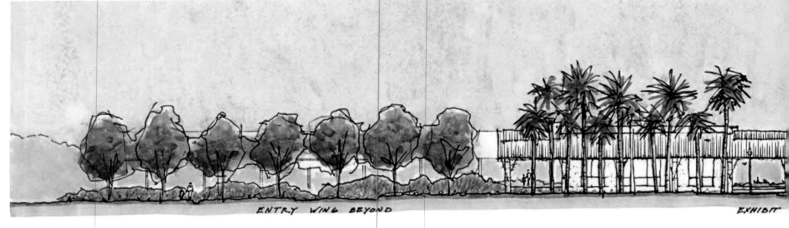

North Elevation

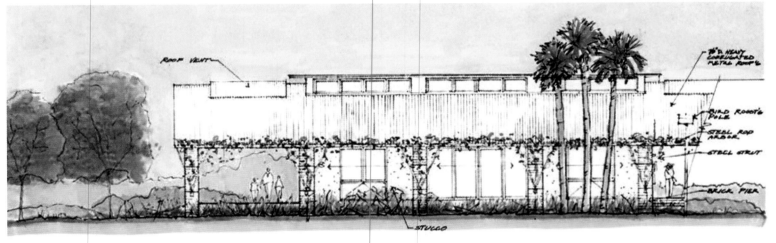

South Elevation

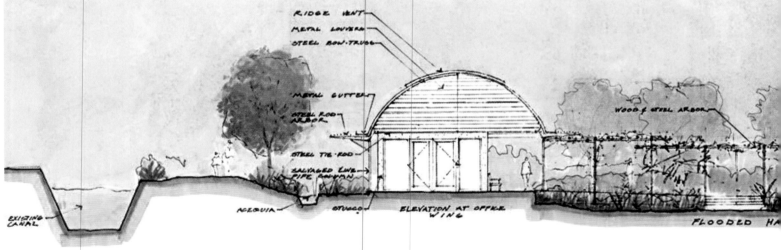

East Elevation

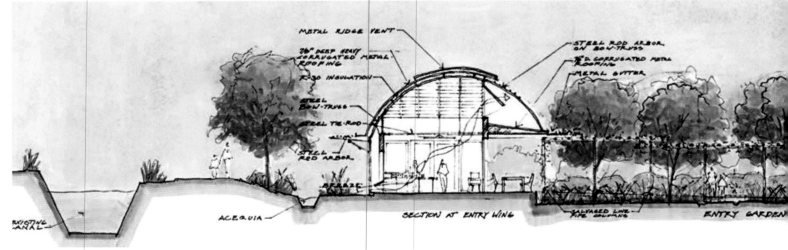

Section at Wetland Court

Breezeways, porches, and arbors link the 32 foot vaults which are both roof and structure.

OFFICE WING BEYOND

36" DEEP HEAVY
CORRUGATED METAL
ROOF

STEEL BOW-TRUSS

STEEL ROD
ARBOR

SALVAGED LINE
PIPE COLUMNS

FLY-ASH CONC.
WALK

STUCCO

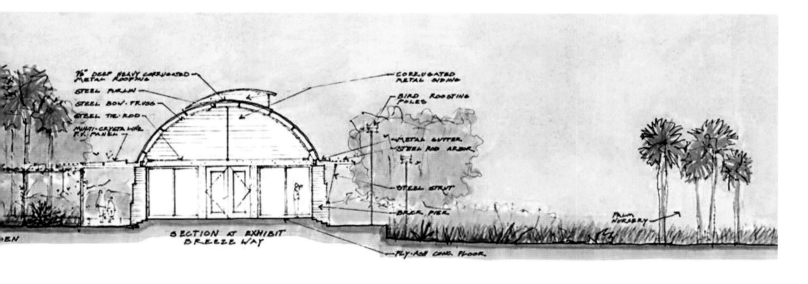

36" DEEP HEAVY CORRUGATED
METAL ROOFING

STEEL PURLIN

STEEL BOW-TRUSS

STEEL TIE-ROD

MULTI-CRYSTALLINE
P.V. PANEL

CORRUGATED
METAL SIDING

BIRD ROOSTING
POLES

METAL GUTTER

STEEL ROD ARBOR

STEEL STRUT

BRICK PIER

SECTION AT EXHIBIT
BREEZE WAY

FLY-ASH CONC. FLOOR

PALM
NURSERY

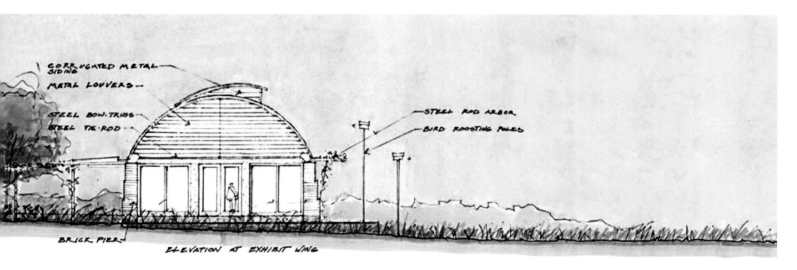

CORRUGATED METAL
SIDING

METAL LOUVERS

STEEL BOW-TRUSS

STEEL TIE-ROD

STEEL ROD ARBOR

BIRD ROOSTING POLES

BRICK PIER

ELEVATION AT EXHIBIT WING

Porches are carved out ot these spaces while the long vaults round up a variety of courtyards to atttract birds.

Long east/west axis vaults encourage cross ventilation and minimize heat gain.

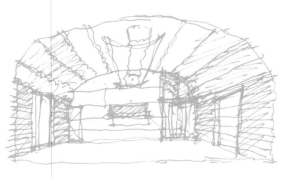

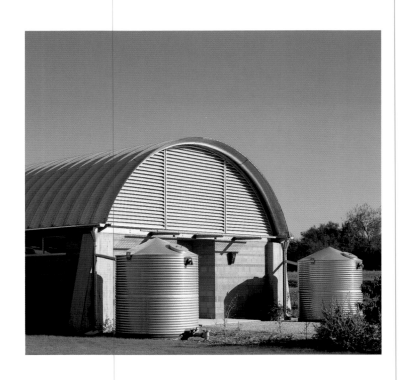

56

Metal cisterns store rainwater; expressed porch vaults frame views.

Local clay tile, salvaged cypress, flyash concrete, and steel vaults double as roof and structure.

Raised arboreal walk takes birders up through the desert to the edge of the Rio Grande River and the raptor viewing platform (opposite).
Helical pier foundation allows concrete-free foundation with the lowest impact upon the site.

COMMUNITY ARENA
In Collaboration with Ellerbe Becket and Kell Munoz

The spectacle of sport provides a high-energy activity, demanding huge amounts of power and acreage. Lake/Flato, inspired by the outdoor fiestas and culture of South Texas, reduced the scale of this big sports arena for the San Antonio Spurs basketball team into a series of porches, loggias, and silos that welcome visitors and mitigate the effects of the climate. Located among the barns and pens of the San Antonio Rodeo site—a hot, unshaded, flat place—this arena fuses the ranch-tech aesthetic of rodeo barns as a practical means of providing shade and shelter. Lake/Flato recessed the building into the ground to reduce the apparent size of this 18,500+ seat arena and added shady porches around its perimeter, while pulling hallways and other pedestrian areas to the outside as much as possible, culminating in corner stairs wrapped in perforated-metal sun-screened silos. Between the arena and the adjacent coliseum, the architects strung cables with sheet-metal panels to shade the "backyard" plaza, borrowing the idea from local cattle yards. Broad overhangs, large tall porches, and generous loggias all contribute to the feeling of airiness, appropriate in this climate and for this sport.

San Antonio, Texas
2003

The design springs from practical agriculture and ranching elements: silos, corncribs, and cattle shade structures.

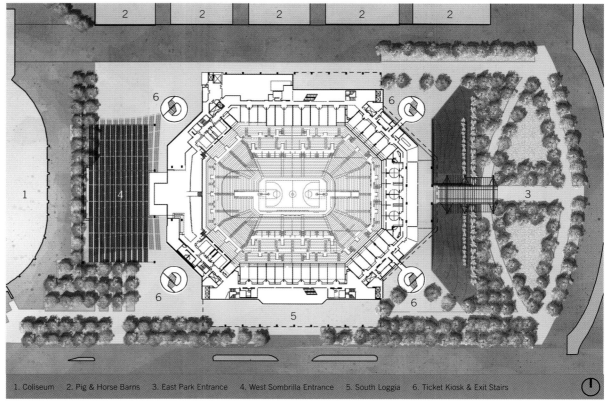

1. Coliseum   2. Pig & Horse Barns   3. East Park Entrance   4. West Sombrilla Entrance   5. South Loggia   6. Ticket Kiosk & Exit Stairs

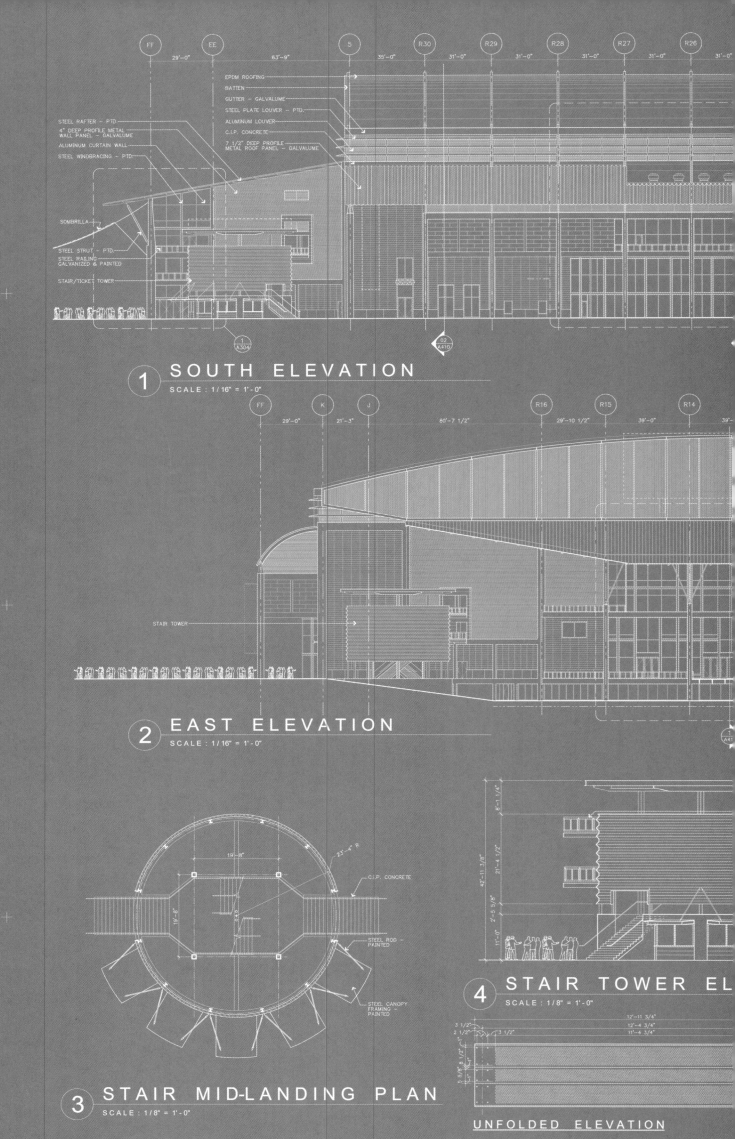

29'-0"   63'-9"   35'-0"   31'-0"   31'-0"   31'-0"   31'-0"   31'-0"

EPDM ROOFING
BATTEN
GUTTER – GALVALUME
STEEL PLATE LOUVER – PTD.
ALUMINUM LOUVER
C.I.P. CONCRETE
7 1/2" DEEP PROFILE
METAL ROOF PANEL – GALVALUME

STEEL RAFTER – PTD.
4" DEEP PROFILE METAL
WALL PANEL – GALVALUME
ALUMINUM CURTAIN WALL
STEEL WINDBRACING – PTD.

SOMBRILLA

STEEL STRUT – PTD.
STEEL RAILING
GALVANIZED & PAINTED

STAIR/TICKET TOWER

1
A304

02
A410

1 SOUTH ELEVATION
SCALE : 1/16" = 1'-0"

FF   K   J   R16   R15   R14

29'-0"   21'-3"   80'-7 1/2"   29'-10 1/2"   39'-0"   39'-0"

STAIR TOWER

2 EAST ELEVATION
SCALE : 1/16" = 1'-0"

19'-8"
25'-4" R
16'-8"

C.I.P. CONCRETE

STEEL ROD –
PAINTED

STEEL CANOPY
FRAMING –
PAINTED

3 STAIR MID-LANDING PLAN
SCALE : 1/8" = 1'-0"

8'-1 1/4"
42'-11 3/8"
21'-4 1/2"
2'-5 5/8"
11'-0"

4 STAIR TOWER EL
SCALE : 1/8" = 1'-0"

12'-11 3/4"
12'-4 3/4"
11'-4 3/4"

3 1/2"
2 1/2"
3 1/2"
5 5/8"
5 1/2"

UNFOLDED ELEVATION

5 TYP. STAIR META
SCALE : 3/4" = 1'-0"

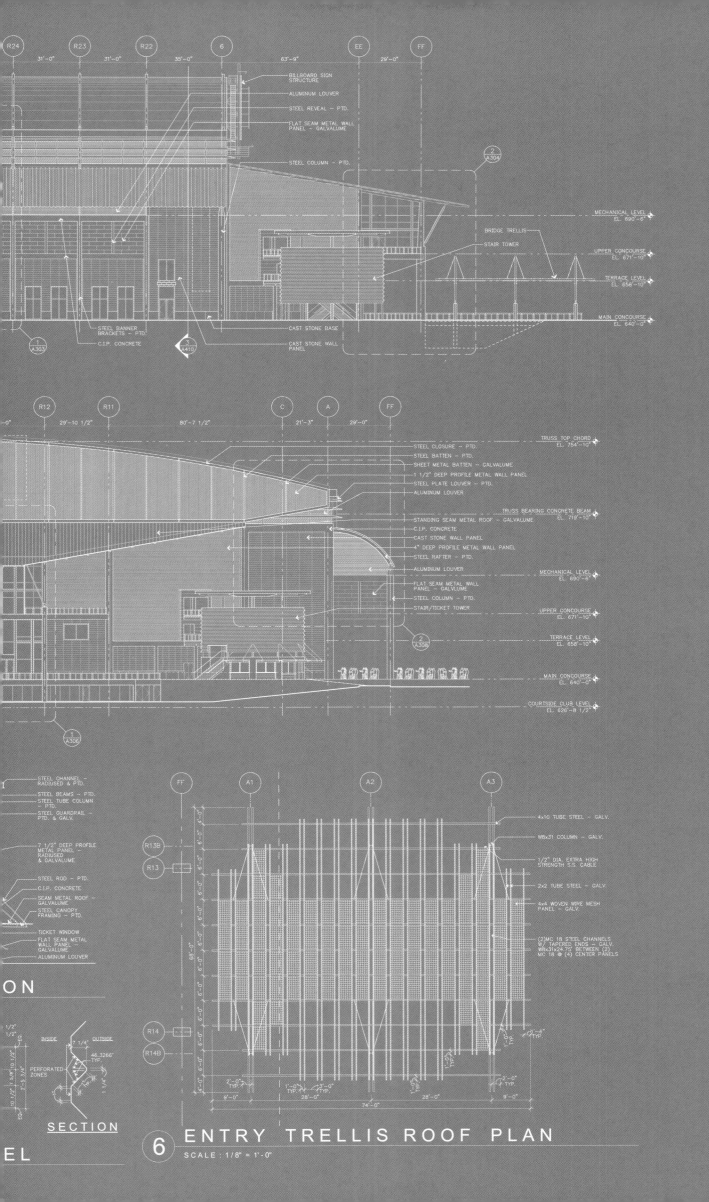

ENTRY TRELLIS ROOF PLAN
SCALE : 1/8" = 1'-0"

SECTION

Porches, arbors, and loggias create shade while the bridge arbor (right) draws visitors through the park to the south porch in a shaded procession from the car to the front door. Breaking up the scale of the roof with vaults, sheds, and silos (below).

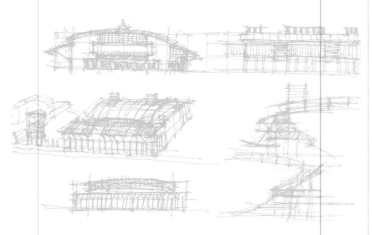
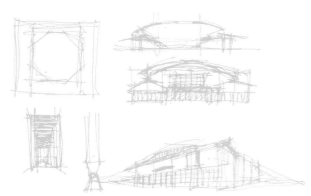

Perforated, corrugated self-supporting metal porches encircle the outdoor stairs to create glowing lanterns and ticket kiosks (right).
The east portal frames views directly into the seating bowl; a lobby mural depicts the historic rodeo roots of the site (above).

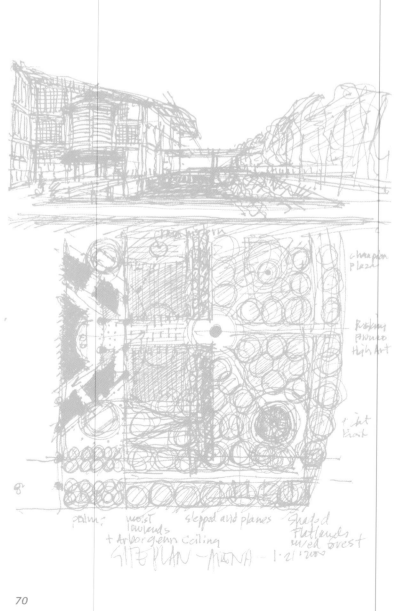

Champion
Plaza

Risking
Bravado
High Art

+ Art
Kiosk

palm: moist   stepped and planes   Shaded
        lowlands   Flatlands
+ Arbor green ceiling   w/ed crest
SITE PLAN ~ ARENA ~ 1·21·2000

Sombrilla Plaza: a great outdoor room shades the western facade and covers the marshalling areas below. Event visitors are welcomed outdoors during events in this secured area. Lake/Flato's masterplan for the 180-acre site created a wooded park entry as a shaded procession to the great porch (opposite).

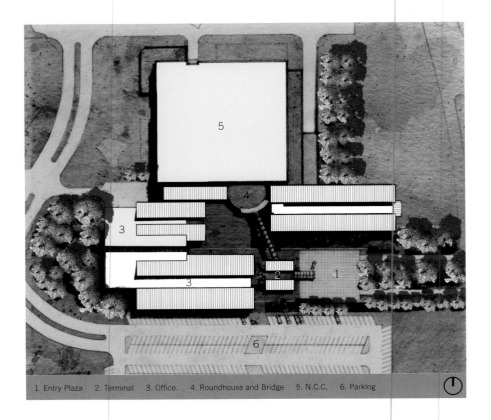

1. Entry Plaza   2. Terminal   3. Office.   4. Roundhouse and Bridge   5. N.C.C.   6. Parking

CORPORATE CAMPUS
In Collaboration with KVG Gideon Toal Architects

Railroads once tied together towns in the middle of nowhere, which is where this railroad company headquarters seemingly sits. On 180 acres at the far edge of Fort Worth, Burlington Northern Santa Fe's campus reflects the rich tradition of railroad architecture, combining the simplicity of Fort Worth's brick warehouses and the prairie's immense concrete silos with the requirements of a high-tech operations center. The architects accomplished this with the grand, round-arched entrance to the building, evocative of the large-scale brick architecture of old railroad terminals. Defining the sides of an automobile forecourt, like lions at the entrance, recycled train cars also block the view of the adjacent parking garage. Seventeen-foot overhanging metal roofs, supported by two pairs of two-story struts, shade the three-story glass window walls of the brick-clad office wings. The long east/west office wings create green courts as refuge from the prairie's sun and wind. The railroad cars, along with other artifacts from the railroads' opening up of the West, capture the essence of BNSF's goal to humanize the scale of this complex, while providing a memorable way of bringing everyone on board.

Fort Worth, Texas
1996

The wide-open prairie site (above right) demanded a campus design with protected interior courtyards (opposite) that contrasted with the expansive landscape.

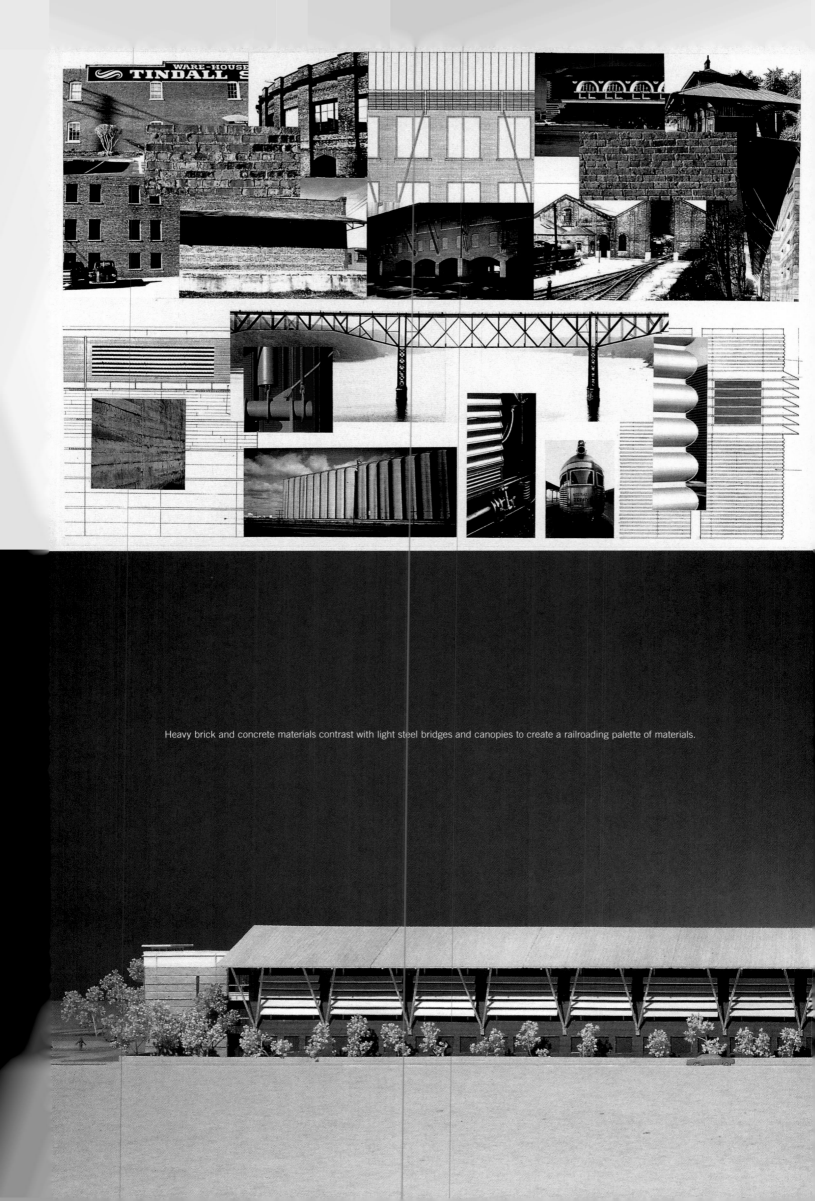

Heavy brick and concrete materials contrast with light steel bridges and canopies to create a railroading palette of materials.

Models of the Terminal Building describe the excitement of entering a great lobby (above).
The long east west buildings maximize daylight minimizing heat and while creating narrow shaded courts (below).

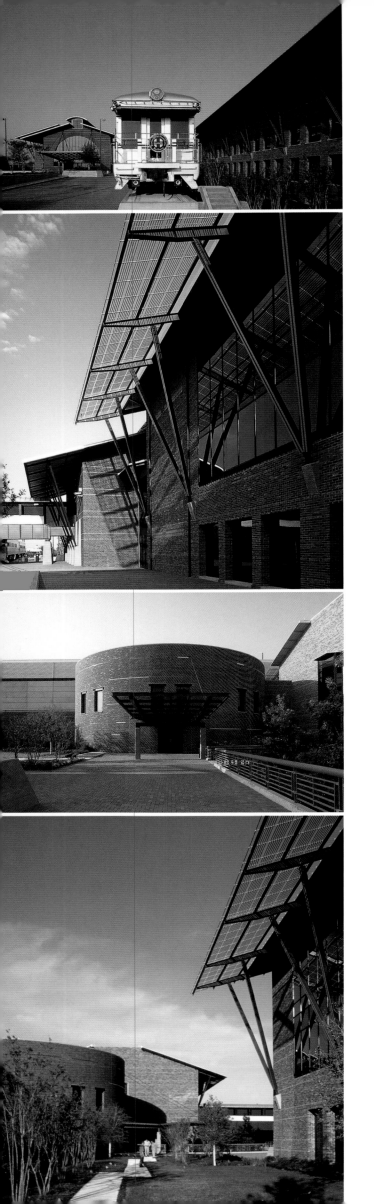

Historic Rolling Stock becomes VIP Conference at the Entry Plaza (bottom right).

Precast beard-formed concrete, mottled brick, light steel panels, struts and bridges create a tactile building palette (right).
Seventeen-foot deep overhangs—solid to the south, open to the north—control glare to allow maximum views (below).

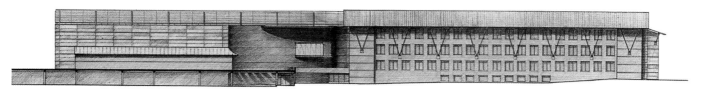

South Elevation Roundhouse Office

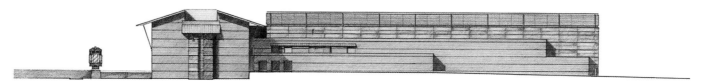

East Elevation NCC

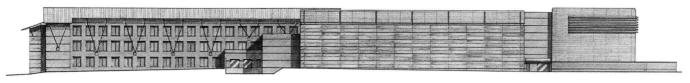

North Elevation NCC

West Elevation NCC

South Elevation Entry Terminal and Office

West Elevation

North Elevation Entry Terminal

East Elevation Office

East Terminal

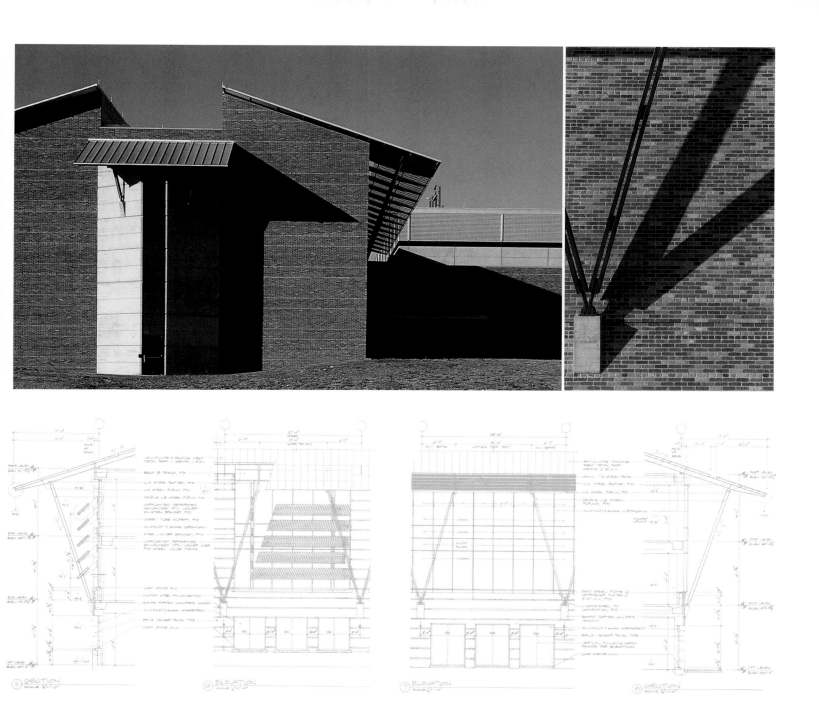

Steel struts support 17 foot overhangs that rest on expressed concrete haunch.

Smooth, precast concrete walls at stairs and control center contrast with the mottled "Burlington Blend" brick walls of the main buildings.

HILLSIDE

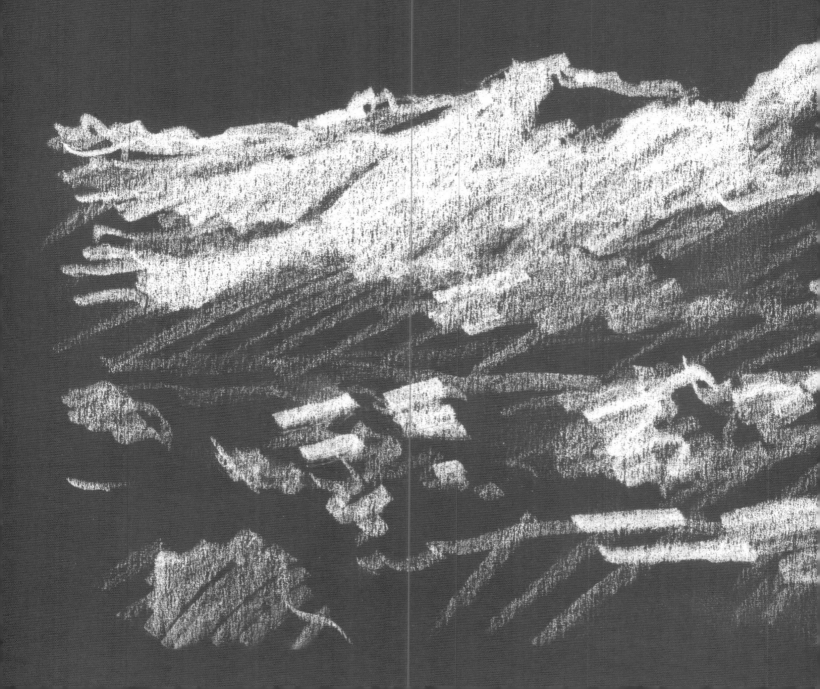

Whether it be on rocky hillside sites, thickly forested slopes, or exposed mountainsides, Lake │ Flato builds in very dramatic landscapes. These places stand greatly exposed, some deep in the woods, but all have stunning views and perches at or near the edges of promontories. In response to these precarious landscapes, Lake │ Flato often accomplishes two goals: anchoring their buildings to the land to provide security and shelter, while opening their buildings out to the vistas that these sites provide. The materials and details of the buildings follow suit. Most have thick stone walls and heavy concrete foundations to lock the structures into the land and expanses of glass set within elegant steel frames to let in light and air, making a seamless connection to the surroundings. The sites shape the plans of the buildings, with some rooms directing you to the far horizons and others looking inward to courts or uphill slopes for a more intimate perspective. In architecture, as in theater, contrast can heighten the sense of drama.

1. Porch 2. Pavilion 3. Kitchen

RIVER RANCH

Perched on a barren limestone bluff in Central Texas, the house melds with the rocky landscape while preserving the natural, sensitive beauty of the cliff. The compact design recalls the simple efficiency of a Bernard Maybeck-designed lodge that Lake/Flato visited in the Sierra Mountains. To accommodate the steep grades and prevailing breezes, the house has a narrow, linear plan. A long, arcing entry porch creates a wide seating area at the midpoint of the bedroom wing and leads, though the kitchen, to the main octagonal pavilion that serves as a comfortable living room and year-round lookout. Weathered limestone collected from the ranch is stacked to create thick, sturdy corbelled piers that anchor the house to the site. Lighter, simpler forms hover among the buttresses and details—such as thin awnings made of recycled oil field rods—lend a delicate grace and contrast with the heavy limestone. In fact, the massive stone buttresses here do as much as the oil pipe shades to provide shelter from the sun while framing living room views to the outside. The cliff-side site may be barren, but the house offers a rich experience of living on the edge.

Mason, Texas
1993

Locally quarried stone buttresses anchor the house to the hill. Pipe arbors shade the western sun.

1. Porch 2. Dogrun 3. Deck

LUCKY BOY RANCH

In the Texas Hill Country, you can live mostly outdoors. Monica and Bob Rivard wanted a weekend retreat on the Llano River. A large breezeway porch serves as the principal outdoor grill and living space, linking the single-story stone-walled public wing with a two-story metal-clad sleeping wing. Above it all hovers a single shed roof that follows the hilly terrain, sheltering the Z-shaped plan and shaping it into a coherent whole. The house responds to its orientation by opening to prevailing southeast breezes, while opaque metal and limestone walls block the cold north winds. This house recognizes the need for a discourse between the man-made and natural worlds, reminding us where buildings began - as shelter from the elements, with a low impact on the site, using mostly local materials. This house suggests that reconnection to nature is the first step in caring for it.

Llano River, Texas
2003

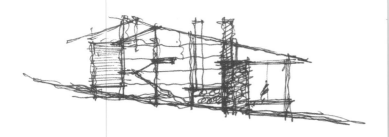

House section sketch (above left). Fort Davis and Dogrun Breezeway (above right). General view from northwest (above).

Retreat designed to be comfortable without air conditioning; porches, dog runs, and one-room design capitalizes on prevailing breezes.

Materials: Drystacked sandstone walls, corrugated metal walls, recycled wood.

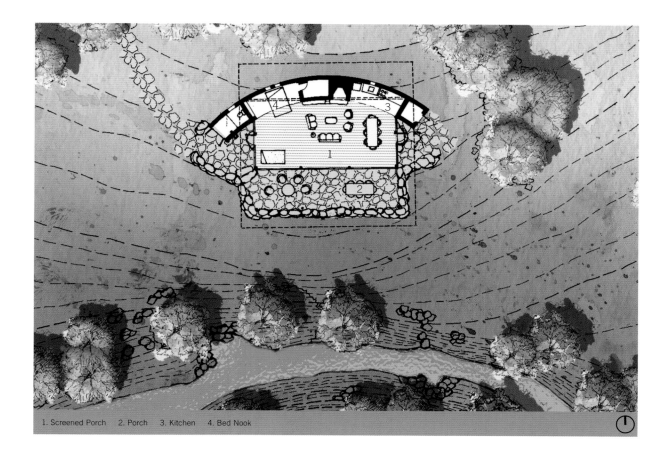

1. Screened Porch   2. Porch   3. Kitchen   4. Bed Nook

LINE CAMP

This is a primitive hut with a purpose. Perched above a stream in the Texas Hill Country, this weekend retreat reduces living to its essentials. Like the local round, stone "stock tanks," this simple, elegant shelter is firmly rooted to its place. The curved stone wall houses the kitchen, fireplace, kids' nook, and outdoor toilet, while sheltering the screened-in living/dining/sleeping space. A broad roof, angled with the slope of the hill, shields the living area from the southeast sun and covers an outdoor terrace. Hinged, wooden panels above the stone wall open to let in summer breezes and close to shut out winter winds. Built from cedar and limestone harvested on-site, the cabin has no electrical or water feeds; the roof collects the rain. The owners, Rick and Kristen Casey, wanted something that sat "lightly on the land" and something that would return to the earth after they were gone. That's living with a purpose.

Bear Creek, Texas
1997

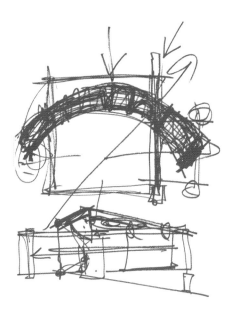

The ubiquitous elevated, round, stone stock tank inspired the design.

Screened porch's stone walls and adjustable flaps block cold winter winds.

The long metal roof collects rainwater, the sole source of water for the house.

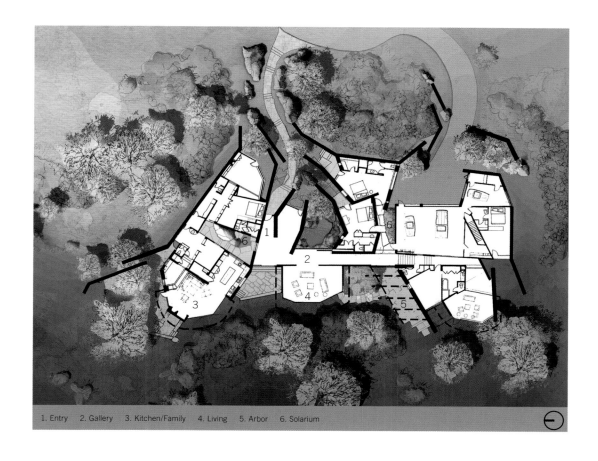

1. Entry   2. Gallery   3. Kitchen/Family   4. Living   5. Arbor   6. Solarium

HOUSE ON A PERCH

This steep site in the front range of the Rocky Mountains dictated a house rooted to the site, while capturing distant views. Fred and Jana Bartlit requested "a house that was seamlessly connected to its environment." Abandoned mining sheds of Colorado and Irish burial cairns covered in sod inspired this house. The house carefully digs into the fragile, steep site. Bounded by locally quarried granite walls anchored to boulders, the private rooms seem to burrow under native prairie sod roofs, while the public rooms occupy light-filled steel-and-glass pavilions, with gently hovering copper-clad roofs, oriented toward the views. You enter the house through a crevice between granite boulders, leading down to a sheltered court, one of a few intimate outdoor spaces hidden from view by shifting and angled granite walls. A long transverse gallery links the public pavilions with the private bedrooms. Two solariums bring light and heat into the indoor gardens deep in the interior, while mist fountains cool and humidify the house. Humans rarely burrow into the ground for fear of darkness, but the Bartlit house shows how sunlit and light-filled burrowing can be.

Castle Pines, Colorado
2001

Irish burial cairn (above left). Construction Crane showing angled stone walls during construction (above center). House entry (above right).

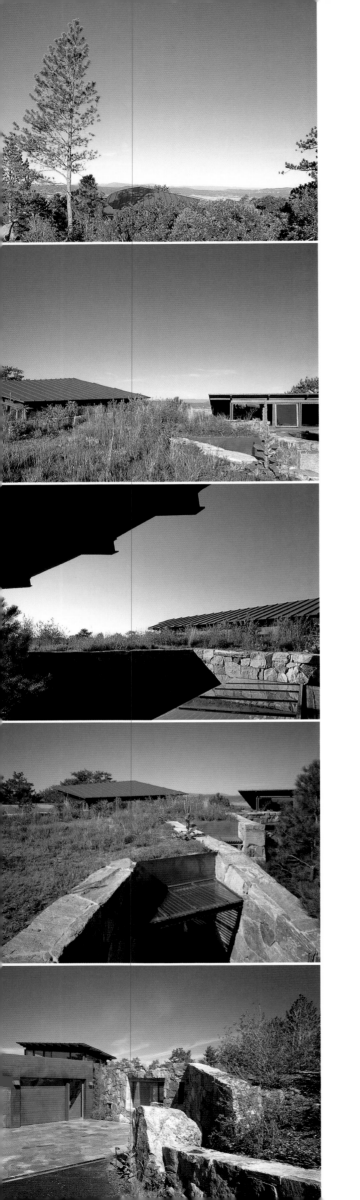

Sod roofs conceal bedrooms; boulders anchor granite walls (right)
22-foot pocket glass doors open to court and fountain.

Light, steel, and glass pavilions contrast with the massive granite walls digging into the site. Cantilevered arbor with perforated copper panels (left).

Solar atrium brings heat and light into center of house; mist garden humidifies arid air; low wood walls conceal closets but accept light.

1. Lobby   2. Bar   3. Dining   4. Kitchen   5. Conference   6. Spa   7. Guest Rooms

GARDEN OF THE GODS

The ancients believed that the gods lived among the mountains and we remain in awe of such sculptural landscapes. This clubhouse and hotel perch on the edge of the cliff fronting the massive vertical red sandstone spires called Garden of the Gods. A great gable roof, with louvered shades and a 15-foot overhang supported by wooden brackets, rises three stories to shelter the lobby, reception, and guest rooms. Taking a cue from the original 1950s clubhouse, a V-shaped porte cochère reaches out with a wing-like roof that looks like it is about to take flight. Inside, the battered walls of locally quarried sandstone, the green slate floors, and the slatted wood surfaces provide warm, cave-like spaces, in contrast to the expansive window walls shaded by an arcing porch. The 85 guest rooms, as well as the spa and conference center, splay out and step back to either side of the central-gabled building, echoing in plan the wing-like roof. If the mountains were once home to the gods, this would have been their garden.

Colorado Springs, Colorado
1997

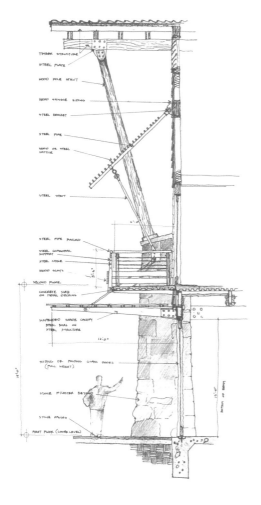

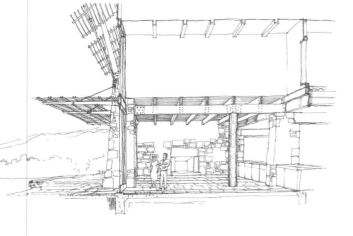

Battered red sandstone piers frame lobby views.
Rustic stone piers, wood struts, and long sheds recall nearby mining structures.

1. Porch 2. Mudroom / Entry 3. Circulation Desk 4. Reading Room 5. Stacks 6. Café 7. Classrooms

SIERRA NEVADA LIBRARY

Buildings often abstract nature, amply evident in this library for Sierra Nevada College on Lake Tahoe. Set in a pine forest with mountains in the distance, the building has a broad roof with bands of dormer windows that rise like outcroppings on a mountain slope. Meanwhile, the heavy timber, exposed-wood frame, supporting wood-sided upper floors and wide eaves, recalls the surrounding column-like trees and their pine needle canopies. Inside the library, a large reading room occupies the main level, with an ascending stair up to the floors of book stacks, enabling readers to re-enact the familiar act of climbing slopes in this mountainous region. Alcoves, projections, and colonnades create visual variety within the overall order of the roof. Nestled into its site, the building conveys the sense of shelter we associate with the forest and with sitting beneath the tree of knowledge within an academic grove. By abstracting nature, this library helps us see nature, and ourselves, anew.

Incline Village, Nevada
2004

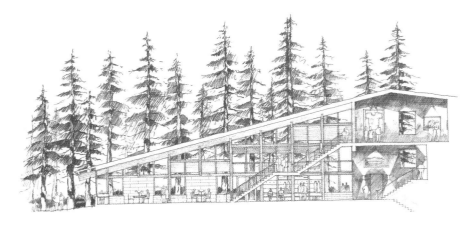

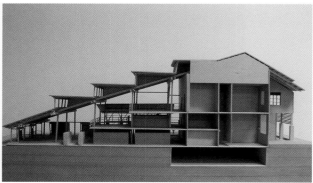

Models and sections of the library showing stepping book stacks and study lofts.

Heavy timber frame and glass infill allow the interiors to connect with the outdoors.

A series of stepping study lofts perched above the book stacks take advantage of the voluminous,
light-filled reading room. As Kahn said: "take the book to the light."

TRANSITIONAL

Transitional landscapes – sites set at the boundary between rural and urban realms – require transitional strategies from buildings as well. Lake | Flato building's artfully abut these landscapes, some of which stand at the edge between dry and wet land, others between natural and residential areas, and still others between busy roads and bucolic settings. The architecture stitches these places together, mending the break between one landscape and the other.

Lake | Flato achieves this by creating clear edges with thick walls or covered walkways to mark the transition, or by designing the buildings to serve as filters with breezeways or courts through which people must pass. At the same time, transitional buildings edit out distracting parts of the environment that disrupt our experience of the natural landscape. While these sites stand at the margin between two different settings, Lake | Flato has made them anything but marginal. You want to occupy and experience these transitions.

1. Entry   2. Gallery/Dining   3. Living   4. Family   5. Arbor   6. Master Suite

HOUSE OF PAVILIONS

Lake/Flato and clients, Garland and Mollie Lasater, began the design process with a trip to Japan to refine their sensibilities about the relationship of gardens to buildings. To enhance the natural characteristics and take advantage of the expansive views of this sloping, wooded suburban site overlooking the Trinity River, the design began with the exterior spaces. The site was broken into a series of "streets" with enclosed courtyards and open spaces defined by walls of native limestone housing the bedrooms and private areas of the house. The streets follow a gradual, open-air descent from the garage and main entry, past private spaces of the house. Glass, copper, and wood public pavilions float above the lush native landscape at the lower end of the site. Sheltered by a series of deep awnings, the pavilions surround the courts and open to views of two distinctively different gardens: a shade garden that works with the large trees and native vegetation, and a garden of soft grasses that overlooks the broad river valley. The planting creeps into the rigorously ordered spaces, softening the planar structures and merging landscapes with buildings, enhancing the sense that the pavilions have naturally emerged from the woods.

Fort Worth, Texas
1994

The gardens of Kyoto had a significant impact upon the design of the house.

Garden-like stone walls conceal the private parts of the house and contrast with the open public pavilions.

The exterior stone walls and paving continue into the inside of the house, creating an indoor street that ties the interior and the exterior spaces together. The paneled, flush oak walls and gapped wood ceilings of the living pavilions contrast with the stone hallway (right).

Landscape architect Rosa Finsley used native planting to create unique garden rooms; vine-covered arbors shade the house. The public pavilions glow at night illuminating the terrace (right).

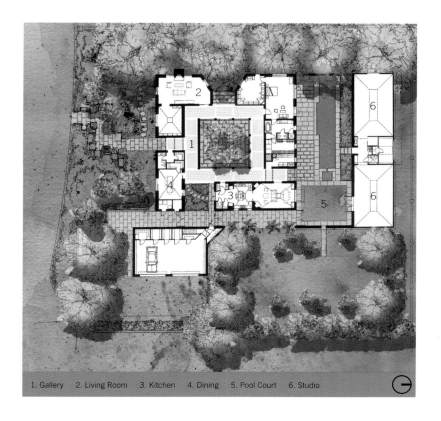

1. Gallery   2. Living Room   3. Kitchen   4. Dining   5. Pool Court   6. Studio

HOUSE OF COURTS

On a suburban street of showy mansions, this house for an art collector offers a lesson in self-effacement. At the front is a low wall of massive stone blocks with a recessed door and vine-covered windows. Inside, a cloister with a glass-enclosed gallery encircles a square, tree-shaded courtyard, with the main living spaces occupying a thick, limestone-clad wall. Cuts in this "inhabited wall" open out to a court facing the adjacent garage, to an existing alley of trees to the west, and to a rear, outdoor pool, with two studio structures peeking above its stone enclosure. Those studios, like several of the living spaces and the second-floor guest room, have ceilings that slope up to glass-enclosed, ventilating cupolas, with broad eaves to keep out the sun. The house is a study in contrasts: the grounded, limestone walls and the light, steel, lantern-like roof hovering above. Like a classic Roman villa that turns its back to the street, this house focuses all of its attentions to the gardens within and creates a place that is far removed from its suburban setting.

San Antonio, Texas
1997

Like traditional courtyard houses, this house turns its back to the street and focuses inward.

Central court's gallery balances daylight with views to outdoors (opposite).

The steel and glass galleries and studios merge with the courtyards while the solid stone walls of the adjacent rooms shield the house from its neighbors (above). Studios have clerestories and cupolas, steel trusses, and framing with exposed acoustic metal decks (right).

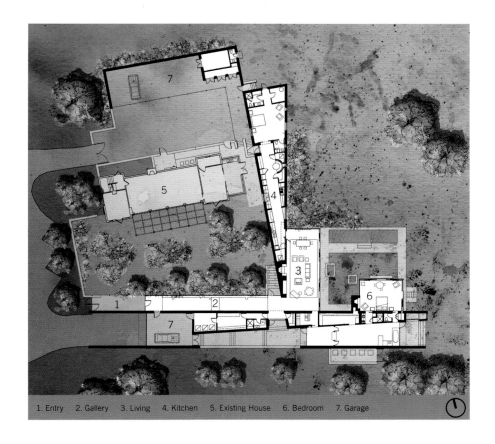

1. Entry 2. Gallery 3. Living 4. Kitchen 5. Existing House 6. Bedroom 7. Garage

EDGE HOUSE

We rarely think of inhabiting walls, but that idea drives this beautifully restrained edge house. Wrapping around an existing carriage house – converted into a gallery and office adjacent to a sculpture garden – the new house consists of two wedge-shaped stone "walls" that serve as the backdrop to two, north-facing, glass pavilions. The glass-walled entry gallery runs along one of these thick walls, which contains service functions such as a garage, storage, closets, and toilets. Another perpendicular wall contains a kitchen and staff quarters. The entry passes through a gap between these two inhabited walls into the large, glazed living/dining room; across a lawn stands a similar glass-enclosed master bedroom entered through the adjacent wall. Both glass pavilions have metal-clad butterfly roofs that funnel water into cisterns, adjacent to a lap pool. All of this happens almost invisibly from the street, where you see only walls, a garage door, and a steel canopy over a pivoting gate. Yet, if the house almost disappears from the front, it and its inhabited walls remain in the memory, like some half-forgotten dream.

Dallas, Texas
1999

Gallery ramps down to the living room (below right). Kitchen designed with a nautical spatial efficiency and wrapped in oak and stainless steel (above).

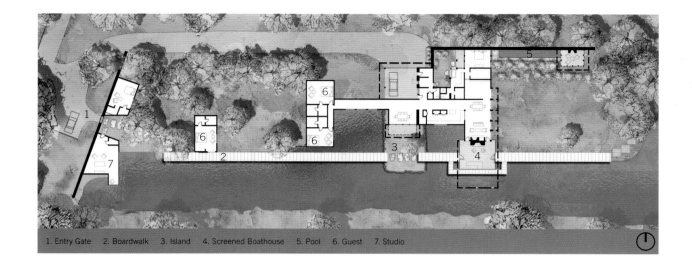

1. Entry Gate   2. Boardwalk   3. Island   4. Screened Boathouse   5. Pool   6. Guest   7. Studio

CANAL HOUSE

Early human settlements usually stood next to water, and that location remains deeply satisfying to us today. In this waterside house, Lake/Flato have designed a "village by a canal," with a series of small, gable-roofed buildings flanking a boardwalk along a Lake Austin inlet. To shield the house on its narrow site from neighbors, the architects have placed limestone walls along the road and property line. A guesthouse and office flank the entry in the roadside wall. From there, the boardwalk extends past two guest-bedroom buildings, over water courts on either side of a dining-room pavilion, to a two-story screened-in living space adjacent to a covered boat slip. An indoor corridor, parallel to the boardwalk, links the bedrooms, carport, and a large L-shaped living/dining/kitchen area. The limestone wall along the property line shields a private court for the master bedroom suite, with a lap pool and pavilion projecting toward the lake. The magic of this house lies in the way it integrates the building and the bayou.

Austin, Texas
2003

A low limestone wall seperates the house from the neighborhood.

Boardwalk leads to screened boathouse; cypress boards clad private rooms and become slats in public rooms.

Copper clad fireplace contrasts with natural cypress walls and framing of main house.

LAKE HOUSE

The desire to live outdoors is an essential part of the design for this house. By pushing the house to the sloping banks of the lake, two different outdoor living areas are created. On the street side is a flat, sunny "play" meadow and on the lake side is the cool, shady, outdoor room. Its main living space consists of a central, octagonal room with large openings to the outside and a central cupola that floods the space with daylight and opens up to augment passive cooling. The room is enclosed by thick walls that house numerous bedrooms and bathrooms within the two-story volume. This room works as the transition pavilion from the sunny meadow to the shady lake and can be opened completely on nice days and closed up for a cold winter or hot summer day. While that room feels outdoors, another room actually is: a large, screened pavilion, connected to the house via a kitchen wing, has its own fireplace for cool nights. Meanwhile, the two guest bedrooms, which hover above boat slips, face each other across an open breezeway that serves as a living room with its own kitchen unit. Most dream of living outdoors; this house makes it come true.

Lake LBJ, Texas
1996

1. Main House   2. Screened Room   3. Boat House

Cupola vents hot air and harvests daylight (opposite). Kitchen opens to screened room.

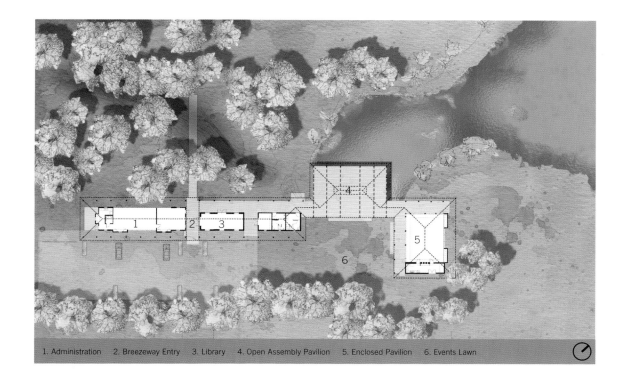

1. Administration   2. Breezeway Entry   3. Library   4. Open Assembly Pavilion   5. Enclosed Pavilion   6. Events Lawn

HILLTOP ARBORETUM

In the past, we spent much of our time seeking shelter in forests, and this arboretum building echoes that sensibility. Acting as a "wall" between the nature preserve and an adjacent neighborhood, the long, single-story building has a pole frame that recalls an alley of trees and a steep metal roof, with skylights that evoke an arboreal canopy. The building's pole structure also recalls the local, indigenous building traditions of old pole barns and columned plantation homes by lifting the interior spaces above the soggy Louisiana earth and protecting them from the damp. The broad-roofed structure shelters three smaller enclosures, two of them – an office and toilets – clad in recycled cypress or metal siding, and a third – a reception area and shop – wrapped in translucent acrylic panels, causing it to glow. At the north end, a hip-roofed, open-air pavilion stands partly in a lake, with a ridge-straddling skylight that makes the space underneath recall a forest clearing. Like the bridge that crosses a ravine to the arboretum, this building elegantly evokes both our connection to and our distance from our half-forgotten, forest-dwelling days.

Baton Rouge, Louisiana
2002

The large steep roof form, indigenous to this part of Louisiana, creates a shaded gallery around the buildings.
Site drainage creates a wetland pond at the pavilion.

The 2x wood framing is expressed throughout the project and is accentuated with translucent acrylic panels.

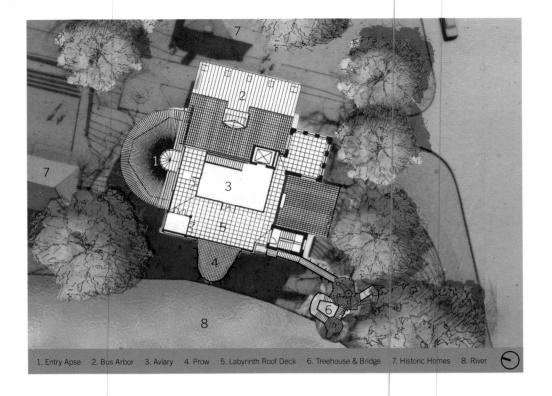

1. Entry Apse 2. Bus Arbor 3. Aviary 4. Prow 5. Labyrinth Roof Deck 6. Treehouse & Bridge 7. Historic Homes 8. River

SCIENCE TREEHOUSE

As children, we often fantasize about ruins, about lost civilizations and hidden treasures. What better idea, then, for a hands-on children's discovery building in a science museum, than a castle, fort, and treehouse, all in one? Director Mark Lane sought a stimulating environment inspired by the tactile and whimsical W.P.A. structures found in the park next door. "Make it as exciting as your grandmother's attic," he said. Standing at the edge of the San Antonio River at the rear yard of the Witte Museum, the H.E.B. Science Treehouse refers to the main building with its stone walls, tile roof, and arches. But Lake/Flato have layered fantasy on top of it in the form of cupolas, spires, crenellations, loggias, balconies, and gangplanks. The rear wall, composed of banded stone piers and glass having an almost Victorian feel, opens out to the neighboring park, while inside, discontinuous stairs encourage a spirit of discovery among children. They can soar like a bird on the prow or burrow like a mole in the underground room. A large treehouse and gangplanks provide another, fantastic way of circulating in and out of the building. This is, without a doubt, the most eclectic of Lake/Flato's projects, and appropriately so. It's for children and for the child in all of us.

San Antonio, Texas
1997

WPA era park pavilions and bridges have an eclectic magic while the Witte Museum's romanesque campus and historic houses create a village.

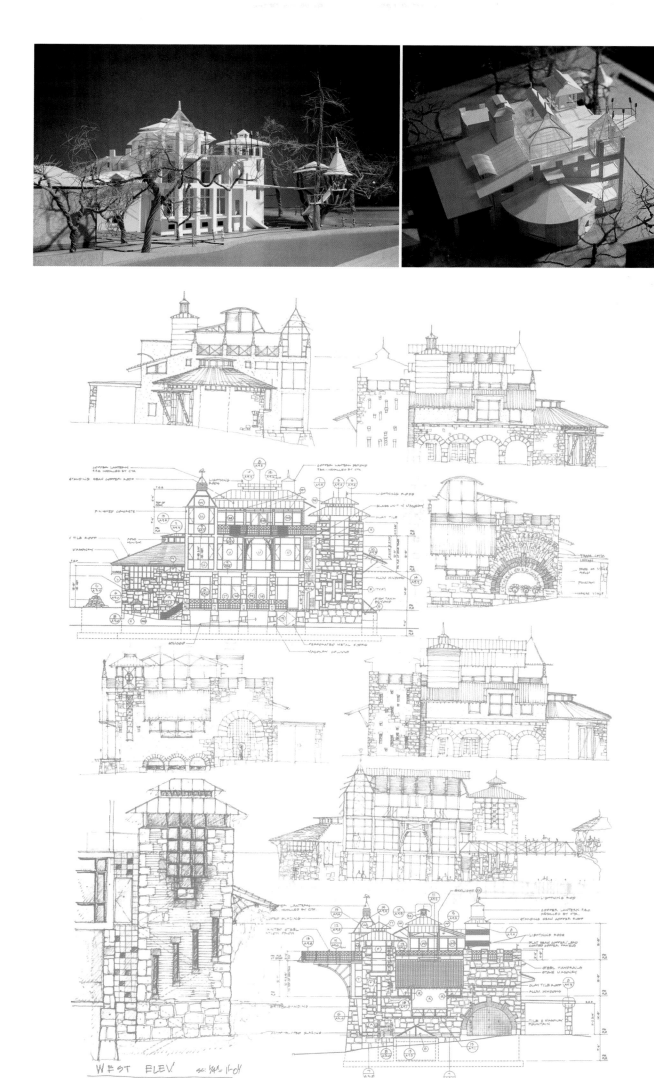

Each facade has a unique character in response to the site.
The striped columns speak to the park buildings while the prow allows kids to fly like a bird.

Limestone, brick walls, and tile roofs match the historic campus.

Each level links visitors to the environment: basement/aquifer room, roof/arboreal room.

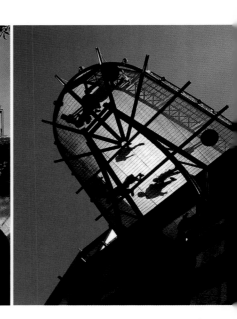

The ferro-cement treehouse holds a busload of kids; local craftsman fashioned the cement to look like a gnarled tree. The waterwheels and archimedean screw are powered by recycled water. The source for the water is the sump pump below the building that intercepts an underground spring. Lake/Flato employees built unique lights.

TEXAS STATE CEMETERY

A cemetery defines a sacred enclosure, which is why this state cemetery, founded in 1851 and located in an old neighborhood east of the Texas Capitol, needed renewal. Urban development had encroached upon the once-rural, 28-acre cemetery, and cars wandered around the site, crisscrossed with roads. Lake/Flato's master plan removed the cars and placed the visitor center and columbarium as quiet, wall-like buildings at the perimeter to provide a sense of enclosure. The visitor center occupies a thick, limestone wall forming a pedestrian portal into the cemetery. The massive stone structure has a calming, tomb-like interior, with low-level openings in the gallery that echo the headstones outside the wall, while the stone floor and dark, wood ceiling create a cool, contemplative refuge. The arcing granite columbarium shields views of neighboring houses, while climbing yellow roses cover a ceremonial, arching trellis framing axial views into the cemetery. Lake/Flato transformed damaging, offsite storm waters into a series of crescent lakes that meander through the wooded draw that traverses the cemetery, cleansing the air with their moving waters. By merging buildings and landscape, the cemetery blurs the distinction between life and death, between inhabitation and internment, creating a sacred ground.

Robert Willson's art (above), traditional walled county cemeteries (above middle), and highway road-cuts (above) played an inspirational role in the design.

Austin, Texas
1997

1. Visitor Center   2. Collumbarium & Hearse Entry   3. Crescent Lake   4. Lone Oak Hill   5. Plaza de los Recuerdos

Sam Houston, Barbara Jordan, John Connally, and J. Frank Dobie are buried here. The columbarium is a linear, walled mausoleum built with rough, asher granite matching the masonry walls at the base of the State Capitol: a sunset red granite from Marble Falls, Texas.
Stone from all across the state was used in the roads and Plaza de los Recuerdos to create a visceral connection to Texas.

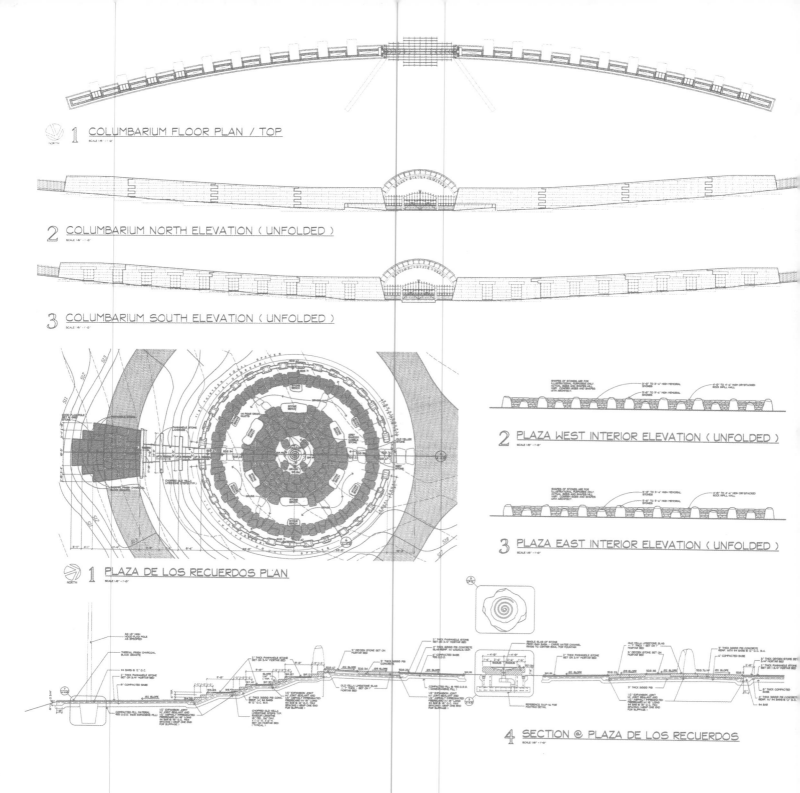

1 COLUMBARIUM FLOOR PLAN / TOP
SCALE 1/8" = 1'-0"

2 COLUMBARIUM NORTH ELEVATION (UNFOLDED)
SCALE 1/8" = 1'-0"

3 COLUMBARIUM SOUTH ELEVATION (UNFOLDED)
SCALE 1/8" = 1'-0"

2 PLAZA WEST INTERIOR ELEVATION (UNFOLDED)
SCALE 1/8" = 1'-0"

3 PLAZA EAST INTERIOR ELEVATION (UNFOLDED)
SCALE 1/8" = 1'-0"

1 PLAZA DE LOS RECUERDOS PLAN
SCALE 1/8" = 1'-0"

4 SECTION @ PLAZA DE LOS RECUERDOS
SCALE 1/8" = 1'-0"

The columbarium, a linear walled mausoleum, arcs toward the entry gate. Plaza de los Recuerdos (Plaza of Memories) is a circle of stones to honor Texans not buried at the cemetery (above). View from visitor breezeway past the ancestral stone to the sacred grounds (right).

TEXAS STATE CEMETERY

Plaza de los Recuerdos: circle of weathered uncut Texas marble with paving from all across Texas (top).
The low openings of the gallery recalls the head stones outside the wall. The limestone wall which was constructed using Confederate monument
bases salvaged during restoration (right).

DALLAS ARBORETUM
In Collaboration with Oglesby-Greene

In gardens, we both admire and tame nature, a paradox expressed in this arboretum visitor education center. The complex has a series of clerestoried pavilions set amidst garden walls that resemble strata of limestone, seeming at once both man-made and natural. Within these arcing garden walls stand the service aspects of the program: gift shop, storage, and kitchen, to the left, and administrators' offices to the right. The walls create an edge and a transition zone between urban Dallas and the pastoral gardens beyond. The arcing form funnels people through a gap in the walls to the plaza, which then spreads out like an alluvial fan into the gardens. Flanking this plaza are the public aspects of the program: large lecture/banquet hall, generous porches, classrooms, meeting rooms, and orientation theatre. These buildings, clad in glass, copper, and cedar, blur the line between garden and building, contrasting dramatically with the earthbound stone walls that establish the "urban" edge. The buildings are designed to be subordinate to the arboretum, and, as the plants mature and slowly take over the building, it will be hard to decipher where the buildings end and the garden begins.

Dallas, Texas
2003

The building design springs from both man-made and natural garden elements.

1. Entry Arbor   2. Gift Shop   3. Exhibit Hall   4. Dining Terrace   5. Plaza   6. Parking   7. Classrooms   8. Conference Room   9. Office

Steps and fountain draw visitors from parking to the entry arbor and garden portal (left).
Sketch shows the gap in the garden wall; the steel and glass arbor is an armature for vines (below).

Arbors are designed to accomodate vines to cover the great porch. Cedar wood walls add warmth to the outdoor rooms.

Sketch plan of the alluvial fan stone paving pattern that draws visitors into the plaza. Quiet education courtyard contrasts with the large plaza (right).

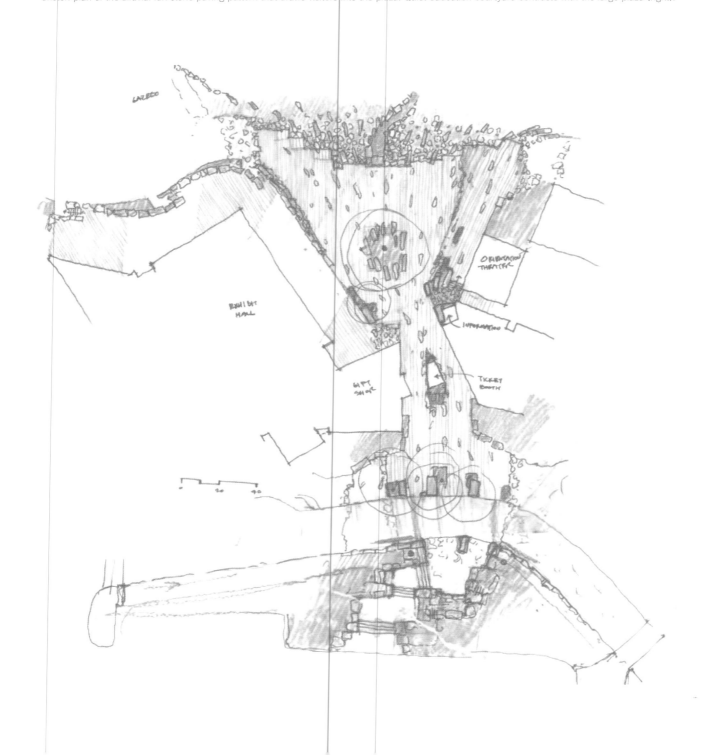

Gabled pavilions hover between stone walls creating day-lit public spaces.

URBAN

Lake | Flato's urban work seeks to repair and maintain civic character while conserving the unique history and eccentric fabric of each downtown. As in rural sites, they provide protected enclosures – a courtyard, plaza, walled garden, and loggia as a refuge from the urban condition. Lake | Flato's buildings create pivotal linkages which improve circulation and access while defining the street edge, connecting and continuing the neighborhoods character or simply greeting the gesture of a nearby structure. Often the site lacks definition, the firm creates an appropriate urban context with a compound; a city in miniature, as if to reacquaint us with what it feels like to live downtown. Their buildings become urban magnets drawing community and urban landscape together, fostering human contact through urban ecology and renaissance.

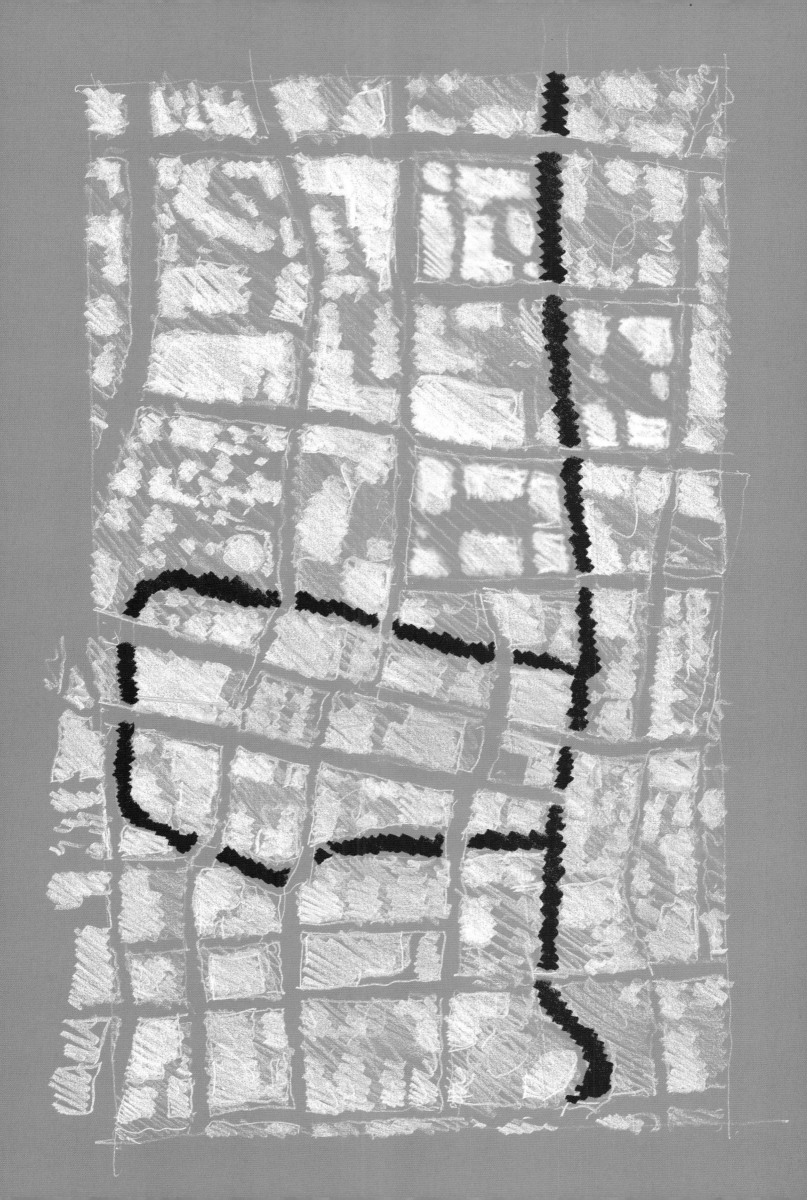

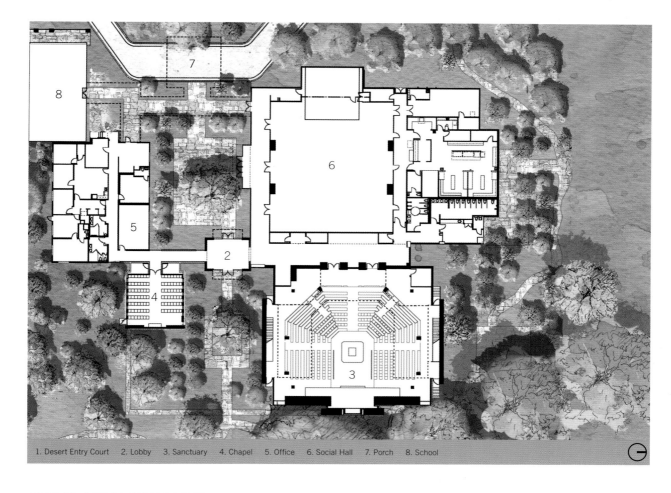

1. Desert Entry Court   2. Lobby   3. Sanctuary   4. Chapel   5. Office   6. Social Hall   7. Porch   8. School

AGUDAS ACHIM SYNOGOGUE

Sacred space does not evolve overnight; it is built over time through ceremony and the honoring of tradition. Lake/Flato sought out the roots of Judaic tradition and began with the first Judaic sacred space: the nomadic tents. The congregation wanted an intimate space, where anywhere from 250 to 1,000 congregants could easily hear the unamplified spoken voice. The architects envisioned a limestone light-filled enclosure surrounding a communal tent-like space. Four concrete columns form an 80-foot square from which a steel structure angles up to form a hexagon 40 feet above the floor. A sky-lit Star of David oculus builds upon the sacred geometries of the Middle East, while clerestories let light slide in behind the cantilevered concrete balconies to glance along dry stacked limestone walls, recalling Jerusalem's Wailing Wall. Wood benches and slatted-wood screens visually warm the space and break up sound, which is absorbed by a quilted, stainless-steel fabric ceiling. All of this gives the sanctuary a feeling of lightness and levitation: a fitting tribute to the legacy of Judaic faith within a modern, light-filled place of worship.

Austin, Texas
2001

A Moorish bath's points of light (above right), early synagogues' nomadic tents (bottom right), sugar warehouses (bottom left), and Gary Cunningham's Cistercian Abbey in Dallas (above left), influenced the architects.

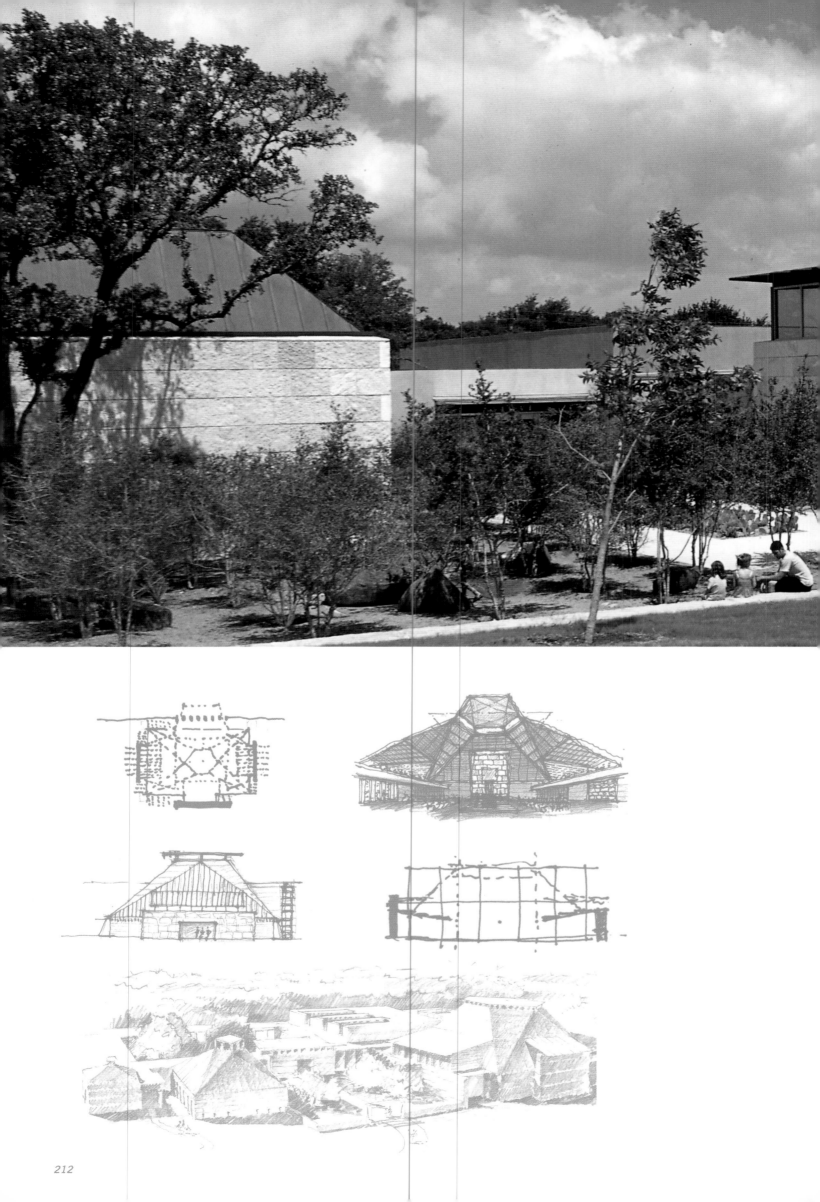

The sanctuary's copper roof contrasts with central Texas limestone; chapel to the left frames the desert court entry. Sketches show the evolution of the tent-like sanctuary space (above).

The sacred geometry of the Middle East inspired the structural framing.
An 80-foot square transitions into a hexagon and Star of David lantern, to create a stone vessel filled with light (left).

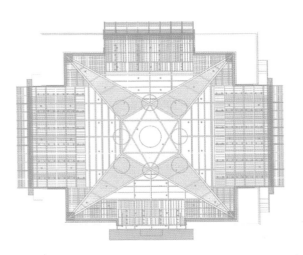

Light slides in between wall and column. Stainless steel fabric, gapped wood walls, and ceiling absorb sound.
Stone walls, solid oak ceilings, and floating shells relfect sound to allow the spoken voice to be heard unamplified.

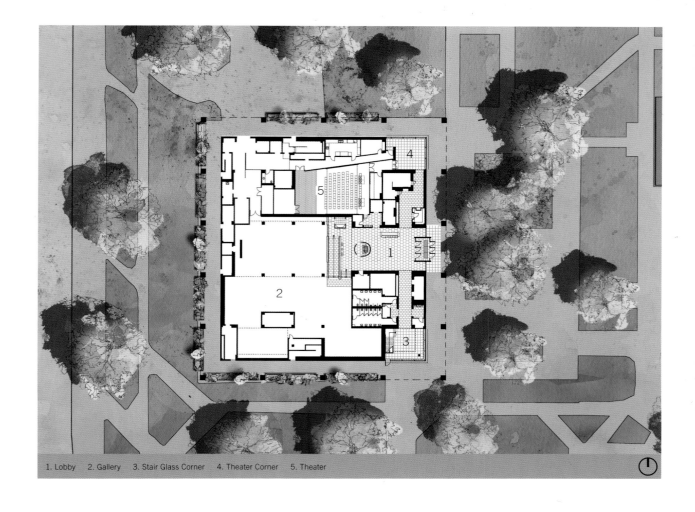

1. Lobby   2. Gallery   3. Stair Glass Corner   4. Theater Corner   5. Theater

CAMPUS MUSEUM

The pervasiveness of information on the Internet has caused once fortress-like archives to become more accessible; Lake/Flato's renovation of the first two floors of this University of Texas archive gives that shift physical form. The original Harry Ransom Center building had mostly blank walls at grade, so much of the renovation involved opening the building to the outdoors. Director Tom Staley requested a reading room, "where the visitor could see trees in all four directions." The architects glazed the entrance and inserted a balcony over the lobby to visually connect the first two floors. They also moved the stair connecting the public floors to the outside corners and glazed its exterior walls with glass, silk-screened with images from the collection inside. The well-lit corner now serves the campus as a lantern at night. Glass in the once windowless reading rooms, corridors, and conference spaces now bring in light and increase visibility, while pecan plywood walls, Texas red granite floors, and brushed stainless steel details make this archive space very appealing. The architects have transformed an introverted library, inappropriate for an Internet era, into an extroverted and elegant campus landmark.

Austin, Texas
2003

Before   After

The stair takes scholars up to the second floor reading room (above). A cut out of the second floor visually links the reading room to the lobby (right).

FD2S and Lake/Flato created distinct panels for each glass facade by selecting images, sketches, and text showing the breadth of the campus museum's collection. The front door features the collection's authors and artists. Aldous Huxley, Hemmingway, Scandburg, T.S. Elliot, Ginsberg et al. effectively sign the entrance and welcome guests. Light and shadow sketches describe the procession through the museum.

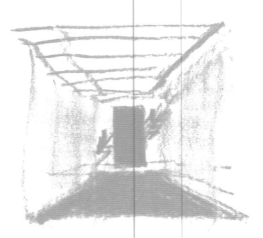

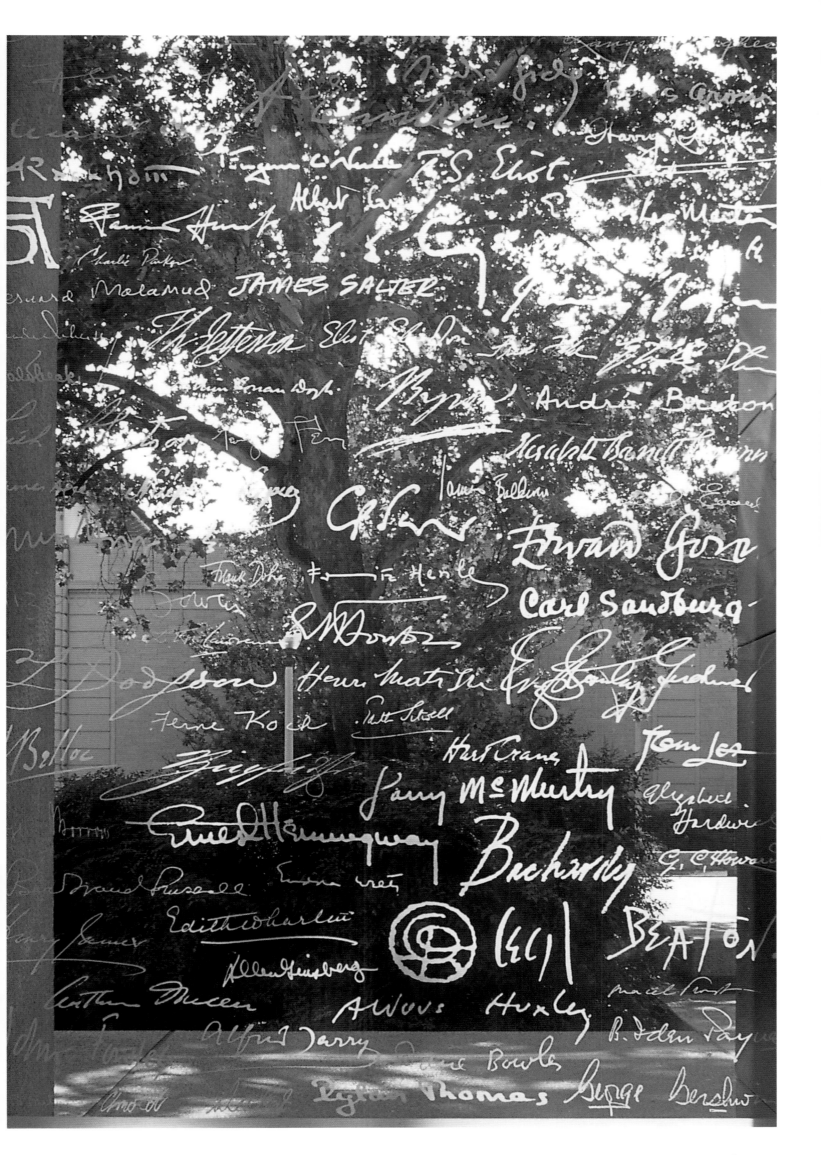

The
Gutenberg
Bible

The Gutenberg Bible, also known as the 42-line Bible, is the first substantial book printed with movable metal type and was completed in 1454 or 1455. The printing process, developed by Johann Gutenberg in Mainz, Germany, allowed multiple copies of a given text to be produced more rapidly and uniformly than was possible with

hand copying. This revolutionary technology accelerated the spread of new ideas and led the way to the Renaissance, the Scientific Revolution, and the Reformation.

Little is known about Johann Gutenberg (ca. 1397-1468). All portraits of him are based on speculation. We know that he was born in

Mainz, lived for some years in Strasbourg, and had some experience working with metals. He experimented with the printing of smaller books before beginning his work on the Bible around 1452. A legal document dated 1455 shows that Gutenberg was sued by his partner, Johann Fust, for the return of large sums of money used in

"the work of the books." This phrase undoubtedly refers to the production of the 42-line Bible.

Gutenberg's wooden press was modeled on the winepress used in local vineyards as well as the papermaker's press. His printing type was made of a durable metal alloy, but exactly how the type was cast and what kind of mold

was used is still a matter of debate. The Gothic letterforms are similar to those used in Northern European manuscripts of the same period.

The Harry Ransom Center's Gutenberg Bible, acquired in 1978, is one of forty-eight surviving copies and one of only five complete copies in the United States.

Between 150 and 180 copies are thought to have been produced. The two volumes include the Old and New Testaments, and the Latin text is that of the Vulgate prepared by St. Jerome. The Bible contains many handwritten additions to the text indicating that it was once owned by monasteries, but we know little about its history before the late 1700s.

The
Gutenberg
Bible

In collaboration with Pentagram, the exhibit designer, Lake/Flato created two enclosures for the campus museum's iconic Gutenberg Bible and the First Photograph.

The machine-age metal box for the first photograph recalls the earliest pinhole cameras (below).

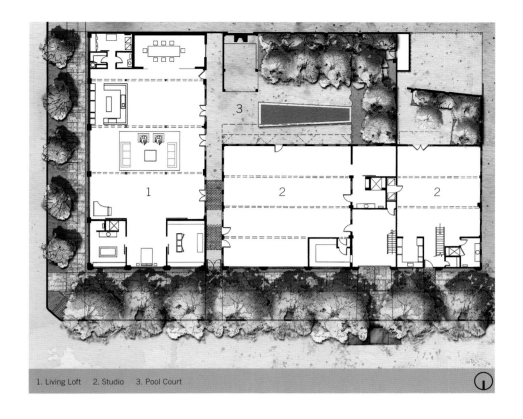

1. Living Loft   2. Studio   3. Pool Court

ALAMO STREET LOFTS

We think of inner cities as tough places, but they are fragile as well, vulnerable to obsolescence and demolition. This adaptation of 1920s inner-city industrial buildings into a loft and studio reveals this paradox by converting a rough factory into a place for generating the gentlest art. Into a corner building severely damaged by fire, Lake/Flato inserted a saw-toothed, steel-framed roof enclosing a large, central living space, with a dining room and bedroom at either end. The raw existing exterior spaces were "tamed" and converted to new uses: the "alley" became the "front entry hall," the "rear parking lot" became the "walled garden pool court," and the freestanding "mechanical building" became the "open pavilion." A second building fronts this court and contains two large studios, guestrooms, service spaces, and garages. "The design," says client Jill Giles, "exhibits a rugged simplicity that took advantage of the good bones of the original building." The materials throughout are tough: exposed steel framing and railings, plaster or exposed-brick walls, and steel-and-translucent-glass cladding infilling the existing brick facades. But that these buildings have survived at all demonstrates what can happen when caring for fragile urban environments.

San Antonio, Texas
2001

Warehouse before restoration.

New Sawtooth roofs bring light and sky into the loft. Stained concrete fiberboard, metal cladding, and fabric canopies add texture to the loft (left).

Concrete floors, wood trusses and skylights, industrial treads and pipe rails.

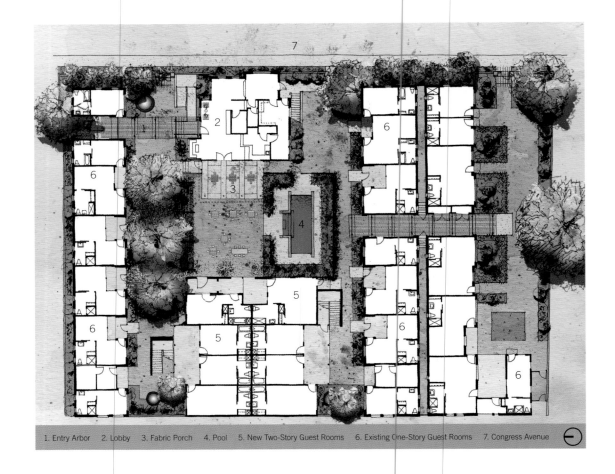

1. Entry Arbor   2. Lobby   3. Fabric Porch   4. Pool   5. New Two-Story Guest Rooms   6. Existing One-Story Guest Rooms   7. Congress Avenue

HOTEL SAN JOSE

Recycling can restore the soul, evident in this recycled 1936 motor court, converted into an intimate, 40-room hotel in downtown Austin. Lake/Flato kept the original hotel office and three rows of existing hotel rooms, combining many into larger suites and converting the carports into private porches. A gray-green color unites the painted brick and natural stucco of the various buildings, while vine-covered cedar wood arbors connect the outdoor spaces once occupied by cars—now filled with a small, bamboo-enclosed pool and heavily planted courtyards. The architects added a 16-room structure at the rear of the old parking lot, mimicking the stucco-and-tile roof aesthetic of the original motel. The central court's canvas-covered porch, pool, and fire pit have become an outdoor lobby, with Outdoor Movies Thursday and Steak Night Friday, making it a community hangout by responding to its original, funky sensibilities. Such eccentricities, afforded by adaptive reuse, have not only transformed an old building, but the street and the neighborhood as well, adding soul to Austin's South Congress Avenue.

Austin, Texas
2000

(Before) Motel overrun with cars and no shade.

Arbors, loggias, and porches lead guests out to an array of courtyards.

Concrete floors, wood slat walls, built-in furniture, and rolling barn doors add texture to this adaptive reuse project.

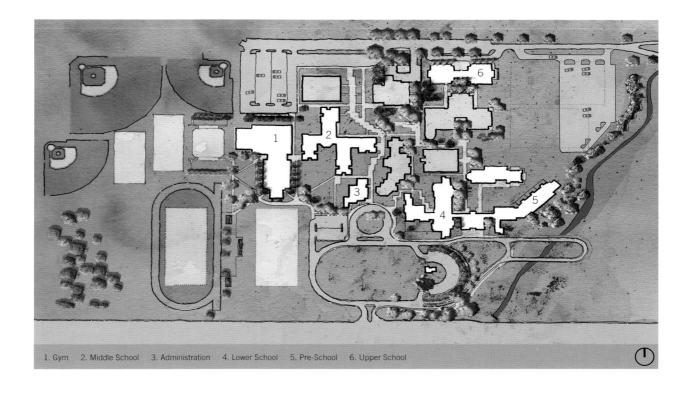

1. Gym   2. Middle School   3. Administration   4. Lower School   5. Pre-School   6. Upper School

GREENHILL SCHOOL
In Collaboration with Hidell Architects

In the build-out of their master plan for this private K-12 school, Lake/Flato have created a more legible series of exterior spaces with a number of insertions and additions to the existing campus. They designed a new administration building with a stepped plan; a repetitive series of chimneys and gables lead students from the circular drop-off into the campus. On the end of each wing of the pin-wheeled Middle School, the architects have added shed-roof classrooms around a clerestoried common space, defining a number of outdoor spaces and connecting the loosely related existing buildings. A central pyramidal roof, topped with a clerestory at the center of the pinwheel, relates to the scale of the adjacent field house, whose bow-roofed gymnasium defines outdoor space and refers to the adjacent athletic fields. To humanize the scale of the exterior spaces, the architects have used climate-responsive details: reflective-metal roofs; deep, bracketed eaves; louvered sunshades, and arcades. In their intelligent arrangement of spaces at Greenhill, Lake/Flato have shown how a campus can be more than its Latin meaning: a field.

Dallas, Texas
Phase 1: 1995 Phase 2: 1998 Phase 3: 2005

The classroom commons links four classrooms (left). Banded brick walls work with the existing campus buildings (above).

1. Entry Porch   2. Office   3. Library   4. Classroom   5. Commons

CARVER ACADEMY
In Collaboration with Kell Munoz

Charity receives little praise in our self-interested culture, but the extraordinary generosity of San Antonio Spurs basketball star David Robinson, led to the creation of this academy for inner-city kids. Working with two historically important civic buildings, the academy consists of a series of four brick-clad classrooms grouped around a common indoor space and courtyard, each connected by a covered outdoor walk that rings a cloister-like quadrangle. A tall trellis and administrative offices mark the entrance into the complex, on axis with the temple-like library, whose broad roof shades the glass pavilion, which is flanked by a cafeteria, computer lab, and science center. The library does not imitate but, instead, compliments and works with the nearby 1930s-era landmark civic structures. The new buildings create a larger campus and strengthen this part of San Antonio's urban fabric. The complex mixes solidity and openness, representing the security and hope that underlie this remarkable institution.

San Antonio, Texas
2003

Urban San Antonio context.

The tall library is the heart of the campus; exterior circulation links kids to the courtyard.

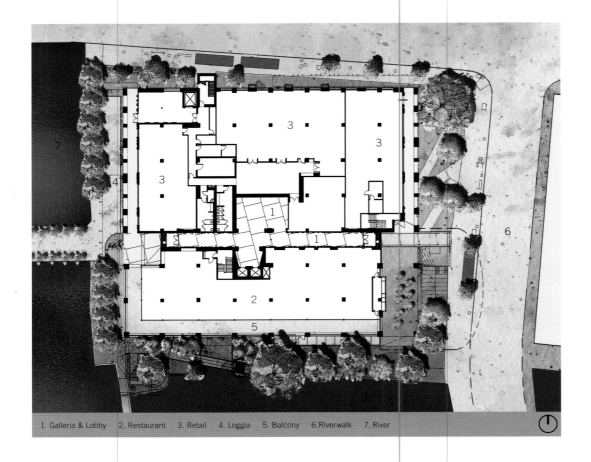

1. Galleria & Lobby   2. Restaurant   3. Retail   4. Loggia   5. Balcony   6.Riverwalk   7. River

INTERNATIONAL CENTER

The renovation of San Antonio's downtown library into a center for trade, tourism, and civic functions provides a unique community asset: a place that connects people to their city and to one another. The 1972 library, an opaque brick box, occupied a pivotal part of the Riverwalk, with the river on two sides, so when the city built a new library, it converted the old building into offices for San Antonio's International Trade and Convention Bureau. Lake/Flato have transformed the library by linking the river to the street, connecting the oldest historic plaza to downtown's business district. A pedestrian street cuts through the building, past an atrium that vertically links the street to the International Center, which now serves as San Antonio's living room. On the Riverwalk side of the building, the architects have emulated the eclectic, back-alley character of the historic river, weaving balconies, terraces, and porches into the exposed structural frame, while the great civic room inside glows at night, like a beacon. The International Center proves that well-designed buildings can be urban magnets, drawing a community together and fostering human contact.

San Antonio, Texas
1997

Existing conditions (above left). Building after renovation (above right).

Riverwalk barges are housed in the lower level marina. The brick skin was removed on the Riverwalk side to accommodate large views and balconies (above). The International Center room is used for trade, tourism, and civic events (right).

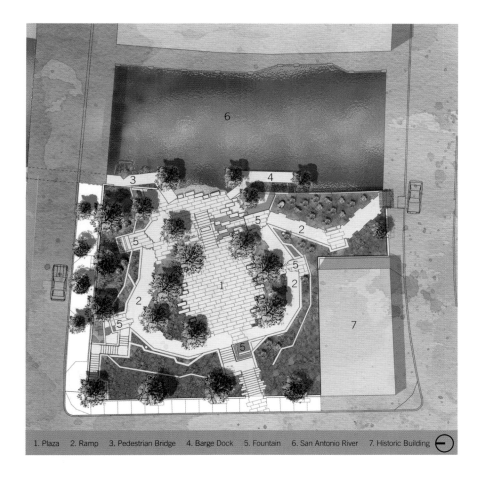

1. Plaza   2. Ramp   3. Pedestrian Bridge   4. Barge Dock   5. Fountain   6. San Antonio River   7. Historic Building

RIVER LINK

Cities tend to forget their origins, but this riverfront park helps San Antonio reflect its past in several ways. Replacing a parking lot, the park connects the main plaza – surrounded by the cathedral, courthouse, and nearby city hall – to the San Antonio River, where the city began. The plaza has broad steps, reflecting the formal nature of the 1700s cathedral nearby, and a meandering ramp, evoking the highly informal WPA-era Riverwalk. The stairs and ramp surround a central plaza framed by cypress trees, part of an extensive native planting scheme designed by landscape architect Rosa Finsley. This new plaza, next to the historical one, recalls the gathering of generations of people at this point along the river. The park also reflects the city's geological origins. Irregular limestone terraces enclosing fountains and pools evoke the river's erosion of the land, while inscriptions, the work of public artist Celia Munoz, recall the history of the city's development. This park beautifully connects not only the city to its river, but also the city to its past.

San Antonio, Texas
2001

Existing conditions (above left). River front park after completion (above right).

A grand limestone stair connects the cathedral and main plaza to the Riverwalk. A series of fountains draw river walk visitors up into the shady plaza.

I WAŚ TAMED, *RÍO AMANZADO*
TO YIELD, TO FEED, TO FOSTER
ME NOMBRARON SAN ANTONIO
WHO FINDS THE LOST

I WAS TAMED, FUI AMANZADO
TO YIELD, TO FEED, TO FOSTER
ME NOMBRARON SAN ANTON
WHO FINDS THE LOST

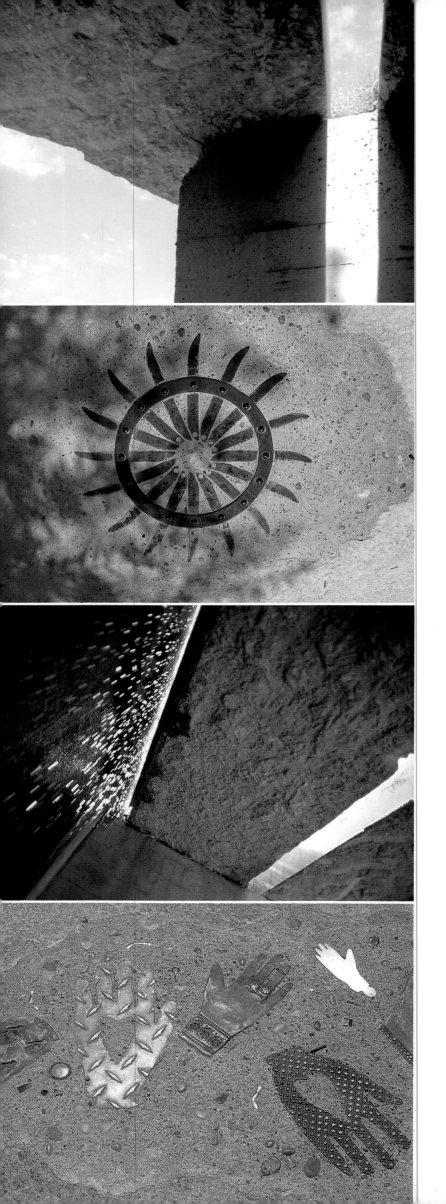

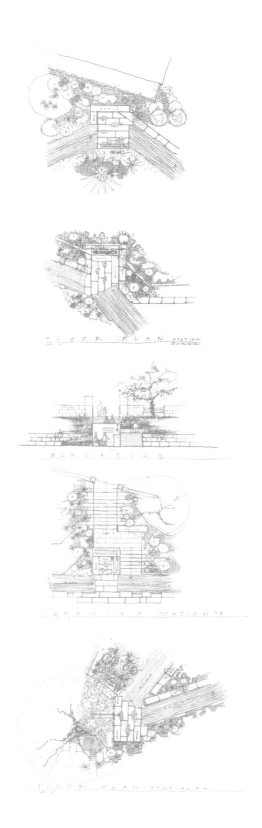

The sketches indicate the various fountains which, combined with "fossils" embedded in the paving, tell a story of the rivers relationship to man (left). Board-formed concrete walls and dry-stacked stone blocks retain the stepped garden terraces.

I RAN FREE, LIKE THE FIRST
HUMAN THAT WALKED ME
YANAWANA WAS MY NAME
PEACEFUL WATERS?

SCHOOL OF NURSING
In Collaboration with Berkebile Nelson Immenschuh Mcdowell

The University of Texas Health Science Center asked Lake/Flato, because of the firm's environmental sensibilities, to create a healthy building for human health: a new School of Nursing. Bob Berkebile and Steve McDowell of BNIM worked with Lake/Flato to assemble a team of environmentally knowledgeable consultants and architects, who were charged with creating a nurturing building. Located on an urban site in Houston, this "vertical campus" has different zones, according to use, that take advantage of the park next door. The most public functions - auditorium, restaurant, bookstore, student services - occupy the park level, with academic spaces in the treetops; the lab and offices rest in the sky. A large breezeway/outdoor lobby links the existing campus buildings to the park and the street. The exterior elevations evolved differently in response to each orientation, maximizing daylight while minimizing heat gain. The fifth elevation, the roof, has saw-toothed roofs oriented to capture photovoltaic production and harvest daylight to illuminate three-story atria at the building's core. Materially, the building makes a statement, built with 50% recycled materials, such as reclaimed cypress, recycled aluminum, salvaged brick, fly ash concrete, and denim insulation, all originating within 500 miles of the site. The School of Nursing has been certified LEED Gold by the United States Green Building Council. This nurturing building proves that balancing the art in architecture with the sciences of engineering and conservation can nurse us all back to a healthier future.

Houston, Texas
2004

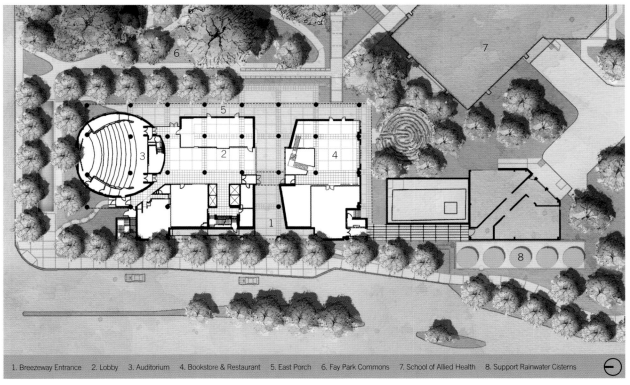

1. Breezeway Entrance 2. Lobby 3. Auditorium 4. Bookstore & Restaurant 5. East Porch 6. Fay Park Commons 7. School of Allied Health 8. Support Rainwater Cisterns

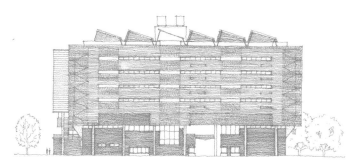

West Elevation

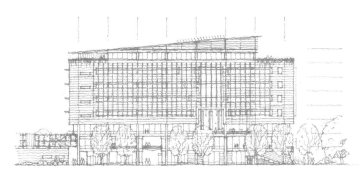

East Elevation

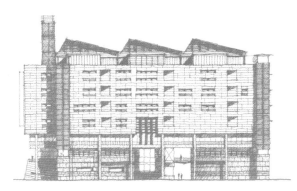

West Elevation

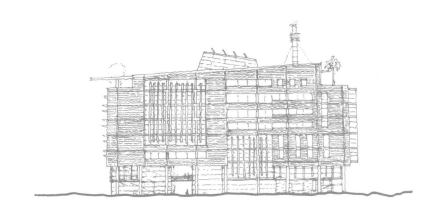

East Elevation

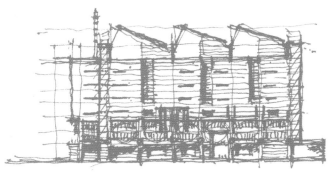

West

East

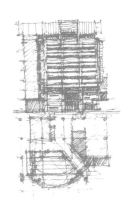

South

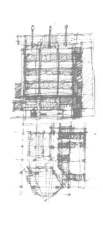

North

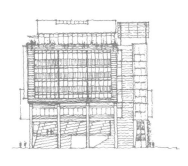

South

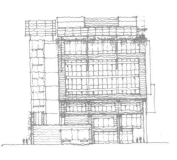

North

The elevations evolved as the envelope became more energy efficient.
The single roof became five roofs in response to the three atria and the need to create a photovoltaic platform.

North Elevation   West Elevation

West elevation's anodized aluminum envelope is
perforated at central stairs to reduce heat gain;
exit stairs are located outdoors to conserve energy.

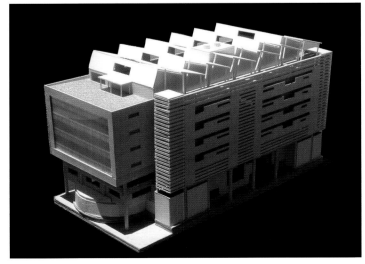

The breezeway links the park to the street. Tensile fabric sunshades bounce light into the office level (right).

The "fabric" of the building is driven by the different solar demands of the various elevations of the building.

East Elevation

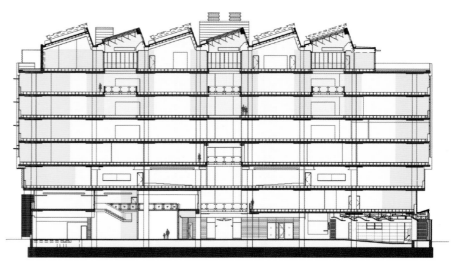

Longitudinal Section

Floor Plan

Daylighting plan and sections evolved in response to the atrium studies. The core was offset to the west to maximize the east floor plan allowing flexibility and day lighting without adding heat load. Computer modeling of the day lighting led to a variety of responses to each orientation. The east façade has tensile fabric sunshades (34% glazed); west façade has perforated metal screens (22% glazed); south has horizontal light shelf/shaders (40% glazed); while the north façade has flush glass (50% glazed). These efforts coupled with a 40% reduction in energy use and an 80% reduction in water use has given this building a LEED Gold rating.

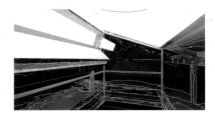
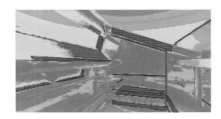

Atrium modeling led to fixed frosted glass louvers to propel light down 3 levels (below right).

Etched glass louvres bounce light into atrium with reduced glare.

"Horizontal" atrium allows light and views to connect two story academic levels.

urban *279*

APPENDIX

ACKNOWLEDGEMENTS

To our clients, friends, and family, who in a number of cases are one in the same. We began Lake/Flato 20 years ago with thin prospects...mothers, sisters, and friends were the only people brave enough to hire us. And to our immediate families, who have been so patient and, hopefully, will continue to be so understanding about hours long gone due to deadlines, competitions, travel, and the daily grind required to fulfill our goals. To O'Neil Ford, the iconoclast and modern Texas regionalist, who we both worked with fresh out of college. He showed us the importance of simplicity and practicality. His greatest gift to us began with an idea he thought amusing: to put two very strong-willed people together on a job that had only room for one and watch the sparks fly! In doing so, O'Neil created not only a wonderful partnership, but an enduring friendship. It has been a long journey from just the two of us to a firm of 50, and a special thanks goes to our partners who joined us along the way and are so critical to our success: Karla Greer, Matt Morris, Kim Monroe, Greg Papay, Bob Harris, Andrew Herdeg, and Associate Partners Bill Aylor, Robert Trinidad, and Brian Korte.

In 2004, Lake/Flato received the prestigious American Institute of Architects National Firm Award and we realized that our greatest contribution to the profession is not our collected body of work, it is our firm of exceptional individuals whose variety of strengths inspire us, and whose camaraderie we seek so we can pursue our rigorous craft with joy...every day.

—Ted Flato and David Lake

Lake | Flato Architects: David C. Lake, FAIA, Principal Edward C. Flato, FAIA, Principal Karla Greer, AIA, Partner Kim Monroe, AIA, Partner Matthew Morris, AIA, Partner Gregory Papay, AIA, Partner Robert Harris, AIA, Partner Andrew Herdeg, AIA, Partner Robert Trinidad, Associate Bill Aylor, AIA, Associate Brian Korte, AIA, Associate Kenneth Brown Paul Schoenfield Javier Huerta Ilsa Korte Jonathan Card Joe Benjamin Brandi Rickels Heather DeGrella Roy Schweers Orlando Ortiz Denise DeLeon Tiffany Gabaldon Elizabeth Dobie-Haynes Jennifer Walters Trey Rabke Tobin W. Smith Kristin Wiese Kimberly Drennan German Spiller Diane Lopez Jo Beth Thomas Heather Weiler Nathan Campbell David De La Hoya Steve Raike Jason Kaseforth Betsy Holt Jodi McCreary Jonathan Smith Tenna Florian Ryan Jones Chris Krajcer Jeremy Fields Cameron Standish John Byrd **Previous Employees:** Graham Martin John Grable Craig McMahon Scott Glenn Billy Johnson, Jr. Jay Pigford Mary Ann Garza Isabel Mijangos Jo Anne Culpepper Darryl Ohlenbusch Matt Burton Joaquin Escamilla Candid Rogers Jennifer Amshey Dale Riser Alix Pillman Lupe Lopez Debbie Means Canan Yetmen Maria D. Garza Greg Snow Francisco M. Lopez Sara Anhalt Karin Shelton Daniel Castillo Janie McFarlane Monty Lee John Nitz Brantley Hightower Marianna Urrutia Robert Maurin Bob Wise Jean LeFebvre Xavier Gonzalez Craig Duncan Andres Gomez Dolores Garza Joe Neely Andrew Clements Jamie Socha Marlayna Brown **Current Interns:** Graham Beach Kayce DeBlanc Williford Tiffany Gabaldon Hollie Scott Elizabeth Graff Stefanie Helfrich Matthew Squire Nikita Payusov Christian Borres Jennifer Young Zeke Freeman Muneera M-Shah Jacob Jay Federico Cavazos **Previous Interns:** Andrej Bissig Alan Knox Alfredo Munoz Christine Anders Caryn Dietrich Charlie Fulton Christopher Kelly Clara Walden Chris White Daniel H. Gonzalez David Munoz Gail Enderle Jennifer Foster Javier Sartorio Jonathan Thompson Kyle Schlie Larry Kunerth Monica A. Garcia Molly Cundari Manuel Esquivel Marianne Ezell Meade Flavin Marcela Gonzalez Michael Kriegshauser Merrick Mycue Margaret R. Sledge Mark Serrata Nathan Bright Noelle Palm Jay Hargrave Nathan Smitson Nathan Wright Parker Atherton Paulina Olin Raul Carmona Rajiv Parikh Sarah Duncan Shelly M. DeVolder Susan Williams Thomas Brown Timothy Britt Toni Souza Vicki Yuan Yolanda Force Abheek Sarkar Cory Dear Lewis McNeel Brent D. Williams Jill Bacon Kwang Hyun Song Ryan Birkley Nick Naeger Nick Rivard Josh Watson Sharon Steiner Chris Vant Hoff Jason Winn Gilbert Sanchez Matt Harvey Craig Bangart aka Stealth Katie Barnes

PROJECT CREDITS

HOUSE OF LIGHT

Santa Fe, New Mexico
Architectural Team: David Lake,
Ted Flato, John Grable, Kenneth Brown
Civil Engineer: Red Mountain Engineers, Inc.
(Jim Kries, Jim Hands)
Photography: Paul Hester, David Lake

DESERT HOUSE

Santa Fe, New Mexico
Architectural Team: Ted Flato,
David Lake, Andrew Herdeg, Roy Schweers
Contractor: Denman and Associates, Inc.,
Landscape: Julia Berman Design
Structural: Red Mountain Engineers Inc.
Interior Design: Sarah Dunning
Photography: Timothy Hursley,
Dominique Vorillon, Erika Blumenfeld

AIR BARNS

San Saba, Texas
Architectural Team: Ted Flato,
David Lake, John Grable, Brian Korte,
Joseph Benjamin
Photography: Dawn Laurel, John Grable

ALAMO CEMENT HOUSE

Kyle, Texas
Architectural Team: Ted Flato,
David Lake, Graham Martin
Contractor: Allen CustomHome, Inc.
Photography: Paul Hester, Undine Pröhl

BIRDING CENTER

Mission, Texas
Client: Texas Parks and Wildlife
Architectural Team: David Lake,
Ted Flato, Robert Harris, Roy Schweers,
Heather DeGrella, Isabel Mijangos,
Javier Huerta, Margaret Sledge
Associate Architect: Overland Partners, Inc.
Structural: Architectural Engineers Collaborative
Mep: ENCOTECH Engineering
Civil: Halff Associates, Inc.
Landscape: Kings Creek Landscaping, Inc.
Contractor: SpawGlass
Photography: Paul Hester, Bob Harris

COMMUNITY ARENA

San Antonio, Texas
Client: San Antonio Spurs and Bexar County
Associates: Ellerbe Becket, and
Kell Munoz Architects
Project Architect: Ellerbe Becket
Architectural Team: Ted Flato, David Lake,
Greg Papay, Kenny Brown, Jay Pigford,
Jonathan Card
Structural: Jaster-Quintanilla
Civil: Pape Dawson
Mep: Goetting & Associates
Landscape: Rialto Studio, Eloriaga Landscape
Contractors: Hunt Construction, SpawGlass
Contractors, Turner Construction
Photography: Paul Hester, Timothy Hursley,
Chris Cooper, Paul Bardagjy, David Lake

CORPORATE CAMPUS

Fort Worth, Texas
Client: Burlington Northern Santa Fe Railroad
Project Architect: KVG Gideon Toal, Inc.
Consulting Design Architect:
Lake/Flato: David Lake, Ted Flato,
Greg Papay, Robert Harris, Robert Trinidad,
Javier Huerta, Francisco Lopez, Enrique
Montenegro, The Pirate John Blood,
Tom Rose, Xavier Gonzalez
Landscape: KVG Gideon Toal, Inc.
Photography: Michael Lyon, David Lake

RIVER RANCH

Mason, Texas
Architectural Team: Ted Flato, David Lake,
John Grable, Robert Trinidad
Client: Mark Chandler
Interiors: June Chandler
Landscape: Jim Keeter, ASLA
Contractor: Henry Duecker
Photography: Timothy Hursley, John Grable

LUCKY BOY RANCH

Llano River, Texas
Architectural Team: David Lake,
John Grable, Javier Saratorio
Photography: Paul Hester, David Lake,
John Grable

LINE CAMP

Pipe Creek, Texas
Architectural Team: Ted Flato, David Lake,
Graham Martin, Brandi Rickels, Eric Buck
Photography: Leigh Christian

HOUSE ON A PERCH

Castle Pines, Colorado
Owner: Jana & Fred Bartlit
Architectural Team: David Lake, Karla
Greer, Robert Trinidad, Bill Aylor, Javier
Huerta, Isabel Mijangos, Francisco Lopez
Structural: Datum Engineers, Inc.
Mep: M-E Engineers, Inc.
Lighting: Fisher, Marantz, Stone Lighting
Interior Design: Gregga, Jordan, Smieszny, Inc.
General Contractor: Beck & Associates, Inc.
Landscape: Kings Creek Landscaping, Inc.
Photography: Paul Hester, Dan Bibb, David Lake

GARDEN OF THE GODS CLUB

Colorado Springs, Colorado
Architectural Team: David Lake, Ted Flato,
Scott Glen, Matt Morris, Kenneth Brown,
Robert Trinidad, Andrew Gomez, Robert
Harris, Eric Buck, Javier Huerta, Francisco Lopez
Interiors: The Hare Group
Photography: Dan Bibb, David Lake

SIERRA NEVADA LIBRARY

Incline Village, Nevada
Client: Sierra Nevada College
Architectural Team: Ted Flato,
Matt Morris, Jonathan Card, Monty Lee,
Isabel Mijangos, Matt Burton
Structural: Datum Engineering Inc.
Mep: Dinter Engineering Co.
Civil: Gary Davis-Consulting Civil Engineers
Landscape: EDAW, Inc.
AV Consultant: Dickensheets Design
Sustainability: Arup
Life Safety: Rolf/Jensen & Associates, Inc.
Photography: Paul Hester, Dan Bibb

HOUSE OF PAVILIONS

Fort Worth, Texas
Client: Mr. and Mrs. Garland Lasater
Architectural Team: Ted Flato, David Lake,
Karla Greer
Lighting: John Bos, Jane & Graham Martin
(Custom Light Fixtures)
Interiors: David Corley
Landscape: Kings Creek Landscaping, Inc.
Contractor: JBM Builders, Inc.
Photography: Michael Lyon, Scott Frances,
Domonique Vorillon

HOUSE OF COURTS

San Antonio, Texas
Architectural Team: Ted Flato, David Lake,
Graham Martin, Robert Trinidad
Structural: Reynolds-Schlattner-Chetter-Roll, Inc.
Interiors: Courtney Walker, ASID
Landscape: Kings Creek Landscaping, Inc.
Contractor: The Hoehler Company
Photography: Scott Frances, Paul Hester

EDGE HOUSE

Dallas, Texas
Client: Lucille "Lupe" Murchison
Architectural Team: Ted Flato, David Lake,
Graham Martin, Kenny Brown
Structural: Goodson Engineering, Inc.
Mep: Comfort Air
Contractor: Tommy Ford Construction
Landscape: Warren Hill Johnson
Lighting: BOS Lighting
Photography: Paul Hester, Tom Loof

CANAL HOUSE

Austin, Texas
Architectural Team: Ted Flato, David Lake,
Bill Aylor
Structural: Lundy and Associates
Mep: Comfort Air
General Contractor: Thompson + Hanson
Interior Design: Denison & Denison
Interiors, Inc.
Photography: Paul Hester

LAKE HOUSE

Lake LBJ, Texas
Architectural Team: Ted Flato,
David Lake, Karla Greer
Photography: Timothy Hursley

HILLTOP ARBORETUM

Louisiana State University,
Baton Rouge, Louisiana
Architectural Team: Ted Flato, Andrew
Herdeg, Brandi Rickels
Structural: Stephens Engineering (Thomas A.
Stephens)
Mep: AST Engineering (David Assaf)
Landscape: Reich Associates
Contractor: MBD
Photography: Neil Alexander

SCIENCE TREEHOUSE

San Antonio, Texas
Client: Witte Museum of San Antonio, TX
Architectural Team: David Lake,
Matt Morris, Kim Monroe, Kenneth Brown
Structural: Reynolds-Schlattner-Chetter-Roll Inc.
Mep: Martin Engineering
Contractor: Guido, Inc.
Lighting: Archilume Lighting Design
Photography: Paul Hester, David Lake

TEXAS STATE CEMETERY

Austin, Texas
Client: Texas Parks and Wildlife Department
Architectural Team: David Lake, Ted Flato,
John Grable, Robert Trinidad, Kenneth Brown,
Francisco Lopez, Javier Huerta, Luis Sierra
Landscape: Jim E. Keeter, Inc.
Photography: Paul Hester, David Lake

DALLAS ARBORETUM

Dallas, Texas
Architectural Team: Ted Flato,
David Lake, Matt Morris, Karla Greer, Candid
Rogers, Andrew Clements, Matt Burton,
Francisco Lopez
**In association with Oglesby/Greene Architects
& Pat Spillman**
Structural & Civil: R.L. Goodson
Mep: Schmidt and Stacy Engineers
Landscape: Naud Burnett & Partners
Contractor: Meridian Commercial, Inc.
Photography: Timothy Hursley, David Lake,
Ted Flato, Matt Morris

AGUDAS ACHIM SYNAGOGUE

Austin, Texas
Architectural Team: David Lake,
Kim Monroe, Matt Morris, Kenny Brown,
Jay Pigford
Structural: Datum Engineers
Mep: MEJ & Associates, Inc.
Contractor: Browning Construction
Lighting: Fisher Marantz Stone
Photography: Paul Hester, Paul Roscheleau,
David Lake

CAMPUS MUSEUM

Harry Ransom Center
Austin, Texas
Client: University of Texas at Austin
Architectural Team: David Lake, Ted Flato,
Bill Aylor, Jay Pigford
Mep: Guerra Engineers
Structural: Jaster-Quintanilla & Associates, Inc.
Graphics - FD2S, Inc
Exhibit Designers: Pentagram
Contractor: Browning Construction
Photography: Paul Hester, Leigh Christian,
David Lake, Thomas McConnell

ALAMO STREET LOFTS

San Antonio, Texas
Architectural Team: Ted Flato, David Lake,
Robert Harris, Heather DeGrella
Structural: Steve Persyn
Mep: Comfort Aire
Contractor: Cox Construction
Photography: Paul Hester, Mary Nichols

HOTEL SAN JOSE

Austin, Texas
Architectural Team: David Lake,
Robert Harris, Isabel Mijangos,
Francisco Lopez
Photography: Paul Bardagjy, Andrew
Shapter, David Lake

GREENHILL SCHOOL

Dallas, Texas
Architectural Team:
Phase 1
Design Architect: Ted Flato,
David Lake, Matt Morris, Billy Johnson,
Francisco Lopez
Architect of Record: Hidell and Associates
Phase 2
Design Architect: Ted Flato,
David Lake, Greg Papay, Javier Huerta,
Kenny Brown, Francisco Lopez
Architect of Record: Hidell and Associates
Phase 3
Design Architect: Ted Flato,
David Lake, Craig McMahon, Javier Huerta,
Joseph Benjamin, Brandi Rickles, Daniel
Gonzales
ArchitecT of Record: F&S Partners, Inc.
Structural: Raymond L. Goodson Jr., Inc.
Mep: Basharkhah Engineering, Inc.
Photography: Paul Hester

CARVER ACADEMY

San Antonio, Texas
Architectural Team: Ted Flato,
David Lake, Greg Papay, Brandi Rickles,
Darryl Ohlenbusch, Joseph Benjamin, Raj
Associates: Kell Munoz Architects
Structural: Cutler-Galloway Services, Inc.
Mep: HMG
Civil: Bain Medina Bain
Landscape: Laffoon Associates
Photography: Paul Hester, Greg Papay

INTERNATIONAL CENTER

San Antonio, Texas
Client: City of San Antonio
Architectural Team: David Lake,
Ted Flato, Greg Papay, Robert Trinidad, Kenny
Brown, Javier Huerta, Francisco Lopez, Isabel
Mijangos, Andrew Herdeg
Associates: Danze & Blood Architects
Interiors: Burton Rose Gonzales
Structural: Jaster-Quintanilla & Associates, Inc.
Mep: HMG & Associates
Civil: G.G.C. Engineers, Inc.
Landscape: Everett Fly & The Sage Group
Contractor: Stoddard Construction Company
Photography: Paul Hester, David Lake,
Yvette McClelland, Leigh Christian

RIVERLINK

San Antonio, Texas
Client: City of San Antonio
Architectural Team: Ted Flato,
David Lake, John Grable,
Darryl Ohlenbusch, Brian Korte
Structural: Jaster-Quintanilla & Associates,
Inc. HDR/Simpson
Civil: Pape-Dawson Engineers
Mep: Lizcano Consulting Engineers
Landscape: Kingscreek Landscaping, Inc.
Photography: Paul Hester, David Lake,
John Grable

SCHOOL OF NURSING

Houston, Texas
Client: The University of Texas Health
Science Center
Associates: BNIM Architects
Architectural Team: David Lake, Ted Flato,
Greg Papay, Kenny Brown, Jay Pigford,
Matt Burton
Structural: Jaster-Quintanilla & Associates, Inc.
Mep: Carter & Burgess
Civil: Epsilon Engineering
Exter Wall/Daylighting: Ove Arup & Partners
Landscape: Coleman & Associates
Photography: Paul Hester, David Lake

LA ESTRELLA RANCH   ROMA, TEXAS   LAKE/FLATO OFFICES   SAN ANTONIO, TEXAS

CARTER RANCH   MILLICAN, TEXAS

PINE RIDGE   EAST TEXAS   COWDEN GALLERY

STORY RANCH   CENTERPOINT, TEXAS

COTULLA RANCH   COTULLA, TEXAS

HOLT CORPORATE HEADQUARTERS   SAN ANTONIO, TEXAS   EXCHANGE / GREENGA

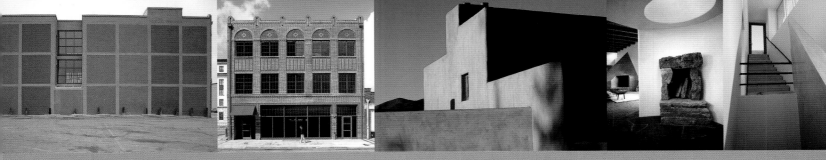

SANTA FE HOUSE I   SANTA FE, NEW MEXICO

TULE RANCH   FALFURRIAS, TEXAS

N ANTONIO, TEXAS   SAN SABA RANCH   SAN SABA, TEXAS   FERNANDES RESIDENCE   MARBLE FALLS, TEXAS

AIR OAKS BANK   BOERNE, TEXAS

AYNE RESIDENCE   MINERAL WELLS, TEXAS

AN ANTONIO, TEXAS   GREAT NORTHWEST BRANCH LIBRARY   SAN ANTONIO, TEXAS   287

PRESENT

INTERNATIONAL MUSEUM OF ART AND SCIENCE   MCALLEN, TEXAS

SAN ANTONIO ACADEMY   SAN ANTONIO, TEX

LAKE TAHOE RESIDENCE   LAKE TAHOE, NEVADA

NOKONAH CONDOMINIUMS   AUSTIN, TEXAS

CANYON OF THE EAGLES   LAKE BUCHANAN, TEX

BROADFORD FARM   HAILEY, IDAHO

LAREDO STATE CENTER   LAREDO, TEXAS

CHURCH OF CONSCIOUS HARMONY   AUSTIN, TEXAS

ARTPACE

PAESANO'S   SAN ANTONIO, TEXAS

RACKEN HOUSE   HOUSTON, TEXAS

SAYRE SCHOOL   LEXINGTON, KENTUCKY

UGHAN RESIDENCE   BLANCO, TEXAS

LE S STEEL   SAN ANTONIO, TEXAS

N ANTONIO, TEXAS   WETLANDS WALK   SAN MARCOS, TEXAS

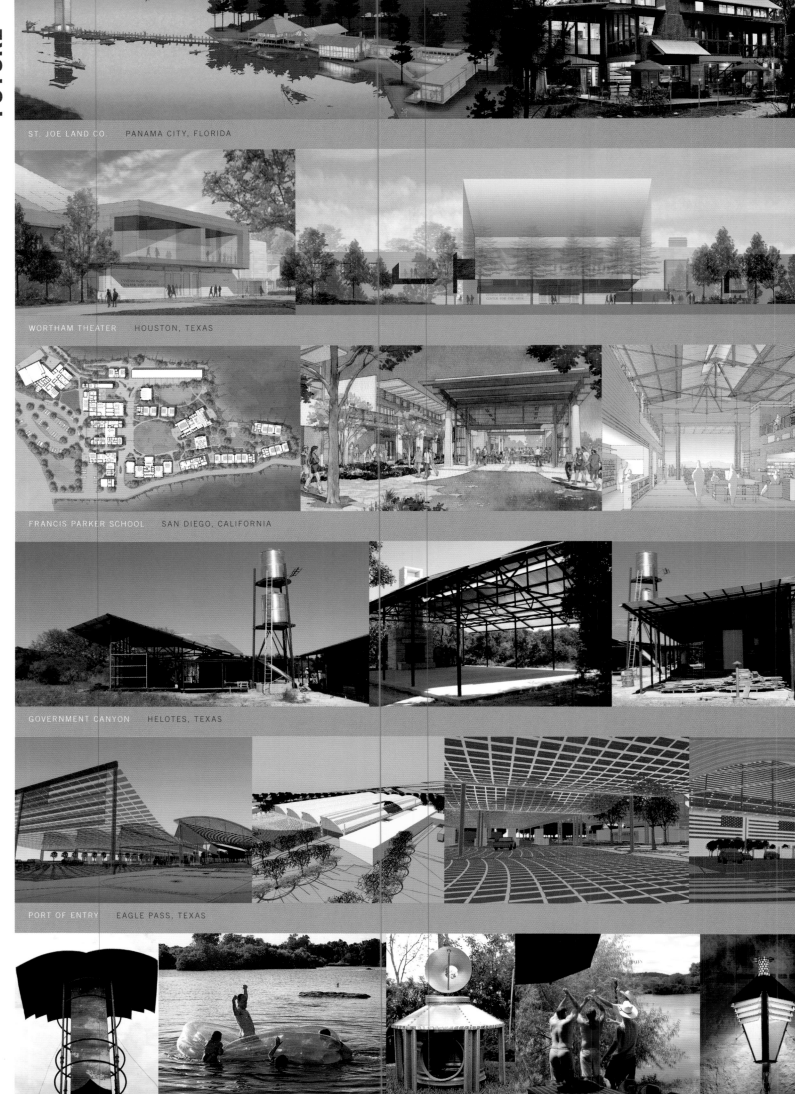

ST. JOE LAND CO.   PANAMA CITY, FLORIDA

WORTHAM THEATER   HOUSTON, TEXAS

FRANCIS PARKER SCHOOL   SAN DIEGO, CALIFORNIA

GOVERNMENT CANYON   HELOTES, TEXAS

PORT OF ENTRY   EAGLE PASS, TEXAS

LAKE/FLATO   FLAKE/LATO: THE ANNUAL RETREAT ON THE WEST NUECES RIVER

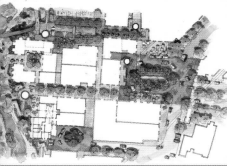

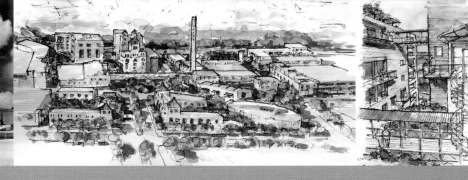

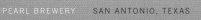
PEARL BREWERY   SAN ANTONIO, TEXAS

LCRA MATAGORDA BAY   MATAGORDA PENINSULA, TEXAS

SHANGRI-LA ARBORETUM   ORANGE, TEXAS

HOUSTON STREET   SAN ANTONIO, TEXAS

OFFICE CRAFTED BATHOUSE, DOGHOUSE, LIGHTS, AND DOGTABLE

COPYRIGHT

FIRST PUBLISHED IN THE UNITED STATES OF AMERICA BY
ROCKPORT PUBLISHERS, A MEMBER OF
QUAYSIDE PUBLISHING GROUP
33 COMMERCIAL STREET
GLOUCESTER, MASSACHUSETTS 01930-5089
TELEPHONE: (978) 282-9590
FAX: (978) 283-2742
WWW.ROCKPUB.COM

LIBRARY OF CONGRESS CATALOGING-IN-PUBLICATION DATA AVAILABLE
ISBN 1-59253-135-0
10 9 8 7 6 5 4 3 2
PRINTED IN CHINA
COVER PHOTO: PAUL HESTER

BOOK CREDITS

CONCEPT: OSCAR RIERA OJEDA, DAVID LAKE AND TED FLATO
PROJECT MANAGER: JAVIER HUERTA
PROJECT COORDINATORS: DENISE DE LEON, TIFFANY GABALDON
PROJECT ASSISTANCE: JENNIFER WALTERS
RENDERINGS: KRISTIN WIESE, JACOB JAY, NIKITA PAYUSOV, JASON WINN, JENNIFER YOUNG, ELIZABETH GRAFF, MATTHEW SQUIRE, ZEKE FREEMAN, STEPHANIE HELFRICH, JONATHAN SMITH
CHAPTER SKETCHES: MATT MORRIS
GRAPHIC DESIGN & LAYOUT: OSCAR RIERA OJEDA (ORO@ORO-ASSOCIATES.COM), IAN B. SZYMKOWIAK (IAN@ALIANDESIGN.COM)
TEXT: THOMAS FISHER
COPYEDITING: ND KOSTER
PRODUCTION: OSCAR RIERA OJEDA
COLOR SEPARATION: UNITED GRAPHICS PTE. LTD., SINGAPORE
PRINTING: SNP LEEFUNG-ASCO PRINTERS TRADING LTD., CHINA
TYPE FACES: TITLES: TRADE GOTHIC BOLD 14PT, BODY TEXT: TRADE GOTHIC LIGHT 9.5/12.8PT, CAPTIONS: TRADE GOTHIC LIGHT 7.5/12PT
ENDPAPER: 170 GSM WOOD-FREE
VARNISH: GLOSS SPOT-VARNISH ON PICTURES ONLY
BINDING: FLEXIBIND

AUTHORS

OSCAR RIERA OJEDA IS AN EDITOR AND DESIGNER BASED BOTH IN BOSTON AND NEW YORK. BORN IN BUENOS AIRES, ARGENTINA, IN 1966, HE MOVED TO THE UNITED STATES IN 1990. SINCE THAT TIME, HE HAS COMPLETED OVER SEVENTY BOOKS, ASSEMBLING A BODY OF WORK WITH PUBLISHING HOUSES BIRKHÄUSER, BYGGFÖRLAGET, THE MONACELLI PRESS, GUSTAVO GILI, THAMES & HUDSON, RIZZOLI, WHITNEY LIBRARY OF DESIGN, TASCHEN, IMAGES, ROCKPORT, AND KLICZKOWSKI. OSCAR RIERA OJEDA IS THE CREATOR OF A NUMBER OF ARCHITECTURAL BOOK SERIES, INCLUDING TEN HOUSES, CONTEMPORARY WORLD ARCHITECTS, THE NEW AMERICAN HOUSE AND THE NEW AMERICAN APARTMENT, ARCHITECTURE IN DETAIL, AS WELL AS ART AND ARCHITECTURE. HE IS VICE DIRECTOR OF THE SPANISH MAGAZINE *CASAS INTERNACIONAL* AS WELL AS A CONTRIBUTOR TO OTHER PUBLICATIONS AND NEWSPAPERS IN THE FIELD.

OSCAR RIERA OJEDA & ASSOCIATES
ARCHITECTURE ART DESIGN
20 CHAPEL STREET, SUITE B702
BROOKLINE, MA 02446
[T] 617 277-8377
[F] 617 277-8366
[C] 617 875-1555
WWW.ORO-ASSOCIATES.COM

THOMAS FISHER HAS SERVED AS THE DEAN OF THE COLLEGE OF ARCHITECTURE AND LANDSCAPE ARCHITECTURE AT THE UNIVERSITY OF MINNESOTA AS WELL AS A PROFESSOR IN THE DEPARTMENT OF ARCHITECTURE, SINCE 1996. HE WAS PREVIOUSLY EDITORIAL DIRECTOR OF *PROGRESSIVE ARCHITECTURE* AND *BUILDING RENOVATION* MAGAZINES.

PROFESSOR FISHER WAS EDUCATED AT CORNELL UNIVERSITY IN ARCHITECTURE AND CASE WESTERN RESERVE UNIVERSITY IN INTELLECTUAL HISTORY, REFLECTING HIS INTEREST IN THE RELATIONSHIP OF BUILDINGS TO THE IDEAS THEY EMBODY. PRIOR TO BECOMING THE EDITORIAL DIRECTOR OF *PROGRESSIVE ARCHITECTURE*, HE SERVED AS ITS EXECUTIVE EDITOR AND ITS TECHNICS EDITOR. BEFORE JOINING THE MAGAZINE STAFF IN 1982, HE SERVED AS A DESIGNER AND PROJECT MANAGER IN ARCHITECTURAL FIRMS AND STATE GOVERNMENT.

HE HAS PUBLISHED OVER 200 MAJOR ARTICLES IN VARIOUS MAGAZINES AND JOURNALS AND SEVERAL CHAPTERS AND INTRODUCTIONS IN BOOKS. THE UNIVERSITY OF MINNESOTA PRESS PUBLISHED A BOOK OF HIS ESSAYS ON ARCHITECTURAL PRACTICE ENTITLED *IN THE SCHEME OF THINGS: ALTERNATIVE THINKING ON THE PRACTICE OF ARCHITECTURE* IN 2000, AND A BOOK ON THE WORK OF ARCHITECT DAVID SALMELA IN 2004. DEAN FISHER IS CURRENTLY A CONTRIBUTING EDITOR OF *ARCHITECTURE* MAGAZINE AND *ARCHITECTURAL RESEARCH* QUARTERLY. HE HAS LECTURED WIDELY AT SCHOOLS OF ARCHITECTURE AND PROFESSIONAL SOCIETIES, AND HAS SERVED ON MANY DESIGN JURIES AND ACADEMIC AND PROFESSIONAL COMMITTEES. HIS TEACHING HAS FOCUSED ON ARCHITECTURAL CRITICISM, ARCHITECTURAL ETHICS, AND ARCHITECTURE AND THE HISTORY OF IDEAS.

"THEIR WORK IS A TRANSPARENT AND POWERFUL AFFIRMATION OF THE PROPOSITION THAT ARCHITECTURE IS MORE THAN A GRAVITY-DEFYING PLAN, MORE THAN INNOVATION, MORE EVEN THAN THE GENIUS OF INSPIRATION AND THE DEFT APPLICATION OF EXPERIENCE; IT IS A PUBLIC STATEMENT OF PRIVATE VALUES THAT NURTURE WITHIN THE FIRM A CULTURE OF EXCELLENCE WHOSE TRAITS ARE AN ENLIGHTENED STEWARDSHIP OF SITE CONFIRMED BY A REVERENT APPROACH TO THE LAND, AND RESPECT FOR TRADITION WHILE EAGER TO EMBRACE THE CHALLENGING ADVENTURE OF BRAVE, NEW IDEAS."
—EUGENE C. HOPKINS, FAIA 2004 AIA PRESIDENT IN RECOGNITION OF THE FIRM AWARD 2004

"LAKE | FLATO IS MUCH MORE THAN AN ARCHITECTURE FIRM. THROUGH THEIR KNOWLEDGE AND INTEREST OF THE NATURAL ENVIRONMENT AND THE BEAUTIFUL LANDSCAPE OF THEIR REGION, THEY HAVE BECOME THE ULTIMATE LEADERS IN THE BATTLE FOR THE ENHANCEMENT AND PRESERVATION OF THE ENVIRONMENT. THEIR EXQUISITE AND UNIQUE WORK EXPRESSES BOTH THEIR KNOWLEDGE OF THE HISTORY OF THEIR REGION, AND THEIR LOVE OF THE LAND. BY STAYING AWAY FROM TRENDS AND FASHIONS, AND BY 'LISTENING' VERY CAREFULLY TO THE LESSONS OF THEIR PLACE, LAKE | FLATO'S ARCHITECTURE HAS